P9-CEG-788

YOUTH AND MISSIONS

Expanding Your Students' World View

Paul Borthwick

VICTOR BOOKS®
A DIVISION OF SCRIPTURE PRESS PUBLICATIONS INC.
USA CANADA ENGLAND

Scripture references, unless otherwise indicated, are from the *Holy Bible, New International Version,* © 1973, 1978, 1984, International Bible Society. Used by permission of Zondervan Bible Publishers.

Recommended Dewey Decimal Classification: 155.5
Suggested Subject Heading: ADOLESCENCE

Library of Congress Catalog Card Number: 88-60220
ISBN: 0-89693-582-5

TABLE OF
CONTENTS

796 89

SECTION FOUR
EXPANDING YOUR STUDENTS' WORLD VIEW
BASIC INGREDIENT #3—EXPERIENCES IN MISSIONS
91

SECTION FIVE
EXPANDING YOUR STUDENTS' WORLD VIEW
RESULTS
139

ACKNOWLEDGMENTS

A manuscript like this is not really the work of an individual but a product of a community at work together. Therefore, I am deeply indebted to the parents, youth, and leadership of Grace Chapel who created the community where most of the observations cited in this book took place.

I am also grateful to the dozens of lay leaders and youth ministry interns who have worked with me. I am thankful for the example that they were willing to set, their desire to learn, and their own commitment to world missions.

I am also especially thankful for my team members who joined me in service in Colombia, Vermont, Newark, Ireland, JAARS, Surinam, West Germany, Kenya, and Zambia. These team members taught much of what appears in the "Experience" section of this book. I am likewise thankful for the coleaders on these teams who shared the joy of new adventures in growth and trusting God with me.

There are several people who deserve special recognition because of their dedicated service in expanding the world vision of others, especially through summer mission teams. Craig Utley, Jake Hoffman, and Bob Yackels stand out because of their tireless efforts in giving up vacation time to lead teams every summer.

I am thankful to Dianne Stephens and Cathy Franzoni for their help in typing this manuscript (and for *forcing* me to learn to use a word processor).

Finally, I am most indebted to my wife and partner in ministry, Christie. As coleader on seven teams and overall affirmer of me and others, I am thankful for her because she provided the needed encouragement to me to persevere, even when no one else seemed to believe that youth could benefit from having expanded world visions.

FOREWORD

I had only been in my first full-time church youth ministry position for six months when I received a phone call one day from a youth minister in suburban Boston. Paul Borthwick was inviting me to join with him and about five other guys for a support fellowship of youth ministers serving in New England. (There were only about six of us doing that youth ministry in New England at the time.) We met once a month for an entire day, studying the Word, praying, sharing (complaining and griping), and enjoying the fellowship of brothers with a common vision and a common calling.

I hadn't expected it when we began meeting, but God used Paul, Dave, Jack, Matt, Ron, and Gerry to dramatically shape and galvanize my sense of commitment to youth ministry.

That was well over a decade ago, but even then, Paul began sharing with us his plans, and his successes and failures, in trying to build into his youth group a world vision and sense of calling. At first, the trips were closer to home—at least by Paul's reckoning: "Yeah, we're taking some of the kids to Yellow Knife in the Northwest Territory of Canada, but I'm hoping to get them to branch out a little more next summer. . . ." Then, there were trips to Morocco, Kenya, Ireland, and the ends of the earth! Using what can only be described as a "biblical neo-Trekkie" strategy, Paul began to equip high school students to "boldly go where no youth group had gone before." It has been exciting to watch God develop this ministry over the years and to see how He has used it to shape and influence young lives.

But this really is the book I've been waiting for. *Youth and Missions* is the culmination of all of these years of mission trips, the experiences, good and bad, together in a book that combines Paul's unique insight for youth ministry with his special ability to put all of this wisdom in a practical format that others in youth ministry can use. This book is just what we need right now in youth ministry.

Every winter, I take some of my youth ministry students from

Eastern College on a trip to Boston during which we interview several people involved in significant youth ministries in that area. I always make a point of taking my students to Grace Chapel in Lexington so that the students can spend time with Paul Borthwick. I want my students to hear what Paul has been doing with youth mission teams over the last ten years.

Inevitably, they sit there, mouths wide open, as Paul recounts tales of various trips hither and yon with his teams of students. I once told Paul that my students respectfully call him the "Indiana Jones of Youth Ministry." Paul laughed, thinking it a big joke.

I smiled at his disbelief, because I know what God has done through Paul Borthwick's ministry over the years, in my life, and in the life of countless numbers of students and volunteer leaders. He has shown them that serving God is an adventure, and that Christianity is not some kind of cheap and easy armchair obedience. It is about taking God's love to every corner of the globe.

My prayer is that this very practical, well-written book will challenge and equip you to call your youth group to that very same kind of wonderful, life-changing adventure. And I also am praying that someday Paul Borthwick and his wife, Christie, will be doing youth ministry somewhere in the shadow of the Great Wall of China!

Duffy Robbins, Chairman
Department of Youth Ministry
Eastern College

INTRODUCTION

It was 1971, shortly after I made a commitment to Jesus Christ during my junior year of high school, that a group from the Grace Chapel youth ministry (of which I was a member) departed for a week of service in the region known as Appalachia. For us, the service project meant assisting in Vacation Bible School in several small towns of southeastern Kentucky. That trip changed my world view.

As an "influenceable" teenager, I was open to learning and discovery, and that trip broadened my view of God, His world, and the needs to which we are called to respond. The trip influenced me so much that in 1977, when I was first given full responsibility for our high school ministry, I began to research how such an outreach team might be formed. The result? In 1978, our youth ministry sent out three mission teams and a stress-camping expedition. I had come to believe that experiential learning was the greatest catalyst for seeing lives changed.

I still believe it over ten years later. We have sent out over sixty youth (and since 1983, adult) mission teams to a variety of locations—both domestic and international. We have had countless missions lessons, dozens of fund-raisers, and scores of missions speakers in our church and at the youth group.

The three basic ingredients offered in this book—example, exposure, and experience—are insights regarding what has worked in the lives of our young people. But they are also personal observations. The example of others who are missions-minded, consistent exposure to missions issues and concerns in my own life, and experiences in short-term mission service projects have changed my priorities, my perspectives, my world view.

As we work to expose our youth group members to the great world into which God has called us as servants, we will face many uncomfortable realities, inequities, and challenges. As we face these, we will choose either to respond or to run. It would be easier to run because many of the issues defy easy answers. "For with much wisdom comes much sorrow; the more knowledge, the more grief" (Ecclesiastes 1:18). The corollary? "Ignorance is bliss."

To respond, however, is the better choice because responding helps us to grow. It is better because it enables us to model responsible discipleship before those we are trying to influence. It is better because to respond is to follow the example of our Lord: "When He saw the crowds, *He had compassion on them*, because they were harassed and helpless, like sheep without a shepherd" (Matthew 9:36).

As we respond, Jesus will give us the ability to see our place and the place of our coworkers in the labors of His plentiful harvest.

I hope that you choose to respond.

TODAY'S YOUTH AND THE
MISSION CHALLENGE

In spite of the abundance of research and writing being done on young people today, teenagers defy generalization. Perhaps the teenagers of the late 80s and early 90s are analogous to a day's activity at JFK International Airport in New York City:
- thousands of planes,
- all high-powered and very valuable,
- all needing direction in order to avoid chaos,
- all headed into very diverse worlds.

How can we respond to such a challenge? Like air traffic controllers, how can we offer the direction to young people that is needed not only to avoid chaos (or disaster), but also to enable them to take off into successful "flights"?

We who are trying to influence young people in churches, youth groups, or youth organizations err sometimes in our efforts of leadership in one or two areas. On the one hand, some of us try to offer leadership and guidance only with respect to spiritual growth. While this may help some students, many others get frustrated because they do not have any tangible outlet for their faith. Barry St. Clair, youth leader and writer, attributes excitement and enthusiasm in a youth group to two factors—"having a growing relationship with Jesus Christ *and being used in the lives of others*" (author's emphasis).[1] If we emphasize only the former, the youth group can grow inward, stagnant, and selfish.

On the other hand, some try to provide a comfort zone for young people in our groups. Rather than challenging them to respond, get involved, and make a difference, we may spend too much time pulling them out of the world that they should help change. Dr. Tony Campolo criticizes this tendency in an article entitled (appropriately) "The Passionless Generation":

> We in youth work have mistakenly assumed that the best way to relate to young people is to provide them with

various forms of entertainment. For many of us, there is
no end to the building of gymnasiums, the sponsoring of
hayrides and the planning of parties. We would do better
if we invited our young people to accept the challenge to
heroically change the world.[2]

If we carried the JFK International Airport analogy over to this
second error, we (as air traffic controllers) would be guilty of keeping all of the planes on the ground. We may indeed prevent any
chance of accidents, but we keep the crafts from accomplishing the
mission for which they were designed.

In contrast to these two errors, our task is to challenge, equip,
and send young people into the "harvest" that Jesus has called us to
(Matthew 9:36-38). To do this, we start by understanding both the
young people whom we are trying to reach and the world into which
we send them. These are the chapters that follow.

NOTES
[1]Barry St. Clair, "They Don't Need a Babysitter," *Moody Monthly* (April 1983), p. 32.

[2]Tony Campolo, "The Passionless Generation," *Youthworker Journal* (Summer 1985), p. 20.

CHAPTER ONE
UNDERSTANDING TODAY'S YOUTH

I have already stated that teenagers defy generalization, but this is not to say that we cannot observe some true patterns about the young people of our times. There do seem to be patterns of behavior, values, and actions that prevail in certain age-groups and in sociological groupings (such as adolescents).

The key for the youth worker is to test these observations against the specific youth with whom we work. For example, I may read certain statistics about teenage behavior in a publication like *Youthworker Update.*[1] Perhaps this newsletter reports that 35 percent of sixteen-year-olds have tried cocaine. If I truly want to understand the issue and how it affects our youth ministry, I must then go to the teenagers themselves. "Is this true in *your* high school?" I will ask. If it is, or even if it is not, I will still get a better understanding of the situation in our community through the resulting discussion.

All of this is to say that the observations which follow may not be completely applicable in every community. Even if they are, the manifestations of the observation may vary widely. For example, some students register their sense of alienation from society by taking drugs, while others retreat to science fiction, music, or even addiction to sports. The wise youth leader is the one that can see the underlying causes of deviant behavior.

I encourage you to test these observations against the young people with whom you work. Some may be applicable; others may not. The critical factor, however, is that we try to understand the teenagers with whom we serve as much as possible so that we can best address their needs and challenge their world views.

Observation #1—Friendship Is Top Priority

I sat with a high school student at lunch one day and asked him, "Dave, who are the leaders at your school?" His response surprised me, having been educated in the school of youth ministry that taught that "peer pressure" and "reaching the influential student groups" were among the two greatest challenges of youth work.

"There are no significant groups," Dave replied. "We all just have our own small group of friends. They are the ones we really care about."

Don Posterski's study of Canadian youth—*Friendship: A Window on Ministry to Youth*[2]—has shown that it is peer group comaraderie that is most important to students today.

> Friendship is center stage for today's youth. As a force, it knows no equal. Friendship is number one as a value; it ranks as the strongest influence, and stands as the highest source of enjoyment in their lives. Friendship is the glue that holds youth society together.[3]

Barbara Varenhorst's pioneer work in peer counseling for teenagers is built on this friendship factor: parents and older adults may not be able to help because they are not the trusted friends. Only those who are peers are considered "real friends."[4]

What has caused this? Is it the increased fragmentation of society that has caused teenagers to withdraw more and more into a small, secure group? Perhaps the increasing stresses in the home have caused some to look elsewhere for security. Maybe the shift toward a small group of friends is a survivalist effort in a world from which many teenagers feel increasingly isolated.

In his study of young people, *When Dreams and Heroes Died,* Arthur Levine summarized the alienation he observed in the following way:

> One senses the development of a lifeboat mentality among students. Each student is alone in a boat in a terrible storm, far from the nearest harbor. Each boat is beginning to take on water. There is but one alternative: students must single-mindedly bail. Conditions are so bad that no one has time to care for others who may also be floundering.[5]

Perhaps young people are turning inward to their small networks of friends because they see the challenges and horrors of the world outside themselves, and they are looking inward for security and safety.

Observation #2—The Future Is Bleak

Although there are some who—for a variety of unusual factors like family, peers, or experience—desire to be world-changers, young people in general seem pessimistic about the future. Thoughts of nuclear war, family breakdown, AIDS, and economic hardship cause fear in many youths.

When I asked Ken, a high school senior, his dreams for the future, he summarized his own perspective this way: "I would like to get enough money to take my girlfriend and retreat to a deserted island in the South Pacific. As I see it, the world is out to get me, and my job is to survive."

Again Arthur Levine's lifeboat analogy comes to mind. Are students really that pessimistic? Do they really see the impersonal "world" as being "out to get them" like Ken?

Perhaps Ken is overstating his case, but there is certainly less zeal these days to change the world and more of a desire to survive or to take care of oneself. Many young people see the future as a void, an abyss which contains only the horrors of war, nuclear destruction, unemployment, and hurt. No wonder students may shy away from service, altruism, or unselfish actions toward others.

In the midst of this pessimism (or in its more drastic cases, hopelessness and despair), the Christian can respond positively because of faith in the God who controls history. This is a challenge, however, because for average students, it will mean a faith that, in some respects, contradicts their own world views.

Observation #3—Students Do Not Integrate Their Faith

The challenge above (hope versus hopelessness) is especially difficult because many students who consider themselves to be Christians have a very difficult time integrating their faith into daily living.

Several high school girls from the same youth group were out one Friday night with their school friends. They went to a movie complex to see a film rated "PG-13." When they arrived, their school friends suggested that they go see a different movie, this one rated "R." The Christian girls offered a variety of excuses as to why they could not go to the "R" movie, most of which were related to their parents wishes. When they were later asked why they did not refer to their Christian convictions as one of the reasons, the girls did *not* say, "We were scared to," or "Our friends don't believe in God," or some other answer that I might have expected. They simply replied,

"That never occurred to us."

Connecting their Christian faith and their movie-going choices "never occurred to them." Why not? These were solid Christians, members of a good youth group, from Christian families. "It never occurred to us." They made no connection between their Sunday faith and their Friday-night choices. These young women reflect many of the teenagers in our churches and youth ministries today.

In our youth work, time must be dedicated to helping students integrate and apply their faith. Perhaps we should use case studies (like those found in *Tension Getters I and II*)[6] to help students apply their faith to real-life situations. We must heed the exhortation of Mike Yaconelli and Jim Burns in their youth ministry manual *High School Ministry*:

> This generation of high school students has grown up in a society that has taught them that faith is a private matter and should not interfere with the public areas of our lives. Because of that, many young people believe that faith is only a *part* of life, not something that influences all of life. The result is that high school students can come to church, be very vocal and involved in their faith, then walk out the door and ignore their faith all week long, *and see no contradiction in their behavior*. The implication for high school ministry is obvious.[7]

Getting young people into missions and service becomes an even greater challenge and opportunity in light of this lack of integrated faith.

Observation #4—Students Are Low on Initiative

Anyone who reads about the sociological observations on young people today will inevitably come across the term "sense of entitlement" in reference to today's teenager.[8] Basically, this phenomenon refers to the affluence with which young people have grown up and which they expect for their own lives—*without* the toil and hardship that their parents expended, of course.

In an angry moment with one of our high school seniors, I was rebuking her for her nonchalance about her college admission test scores and her applications for schools. "You act like you expect the world to be offered you on a silver platter, Pam!"

She replied smugly, "I do."

As I thought of her upbringing, her family, and the affluence she had already experienced, I realized that she believed what she was saying. I knew that Pam would either continue to be insulated by her doting parents or she would soon come to a rude awakening about the harsh realities of adult life.

This "sense of entitlement" leads to lack of initiative, low desire for leadership, and a tendency toward apathy. It may be more and more difficult to get students involved in activities if they are not satisfied with their "what's in it for me?" inquiries. "Meism" is still alive in the youth culture today (as it is in all of Western culture).

Observation #5—Students Desire Independence

Although growing toward independence has always been part of the adolescent "growing-up" process, it has taken a different shape these days. The ever-increasing acceptance of relativistic thinking has led to a generation of young people who desire not only independence from parents but also independence from any absolutes.

Certainly this is not just a teen phenomenon; it affects every part of our culture. Even death itself—the final authority to which life must succumb—has been relativized through the "New Age" teaching of reincarnation. We resist being bound by absolutes, so we invent theologies that (we think) break the bonds.

This drive for independence will create a major challenge for youth workers, for we struggle with the question, When is independence a healthy sign of growth, and when is it outright rebellion? Don Posterski says, "Religion is often viewed as an enemy of freedom. In the perception of many, God has an anti-freedom reputation."[9]

When the topic of world missions is addressed, the relativistic world out of which our students come will lead to the inevitable question, "Well, you're not saying that Muslims, Hindus, Buddhists, animists, etc., are really *lost*, are you?"

If we do not think our youth are affected by our culture's animosity to absolutes, we need only start quoting John 14:6 as an answer to the "What about the fate of those who have never heard?" question.

Observation #6—Students are Pragmatic

Relativistic thinking and nonintegrated faith often times reduce Christian faith in our young people to a personal "it works for me" relationship with God. "If it works, I believe it."

This pragmatic outlook on life has good and bad overtones in the lives of our students as we present to them the challenge of becoming involved in missions. On the good side, they may get very excited about serving because it makes them feel close to God, helpful to others, or useful to the church. In short, they will conclude, "Missions/service is good because it makes me feel good about myself."

While these positive feelings may serve as good motivators, they are pragmatic to a dangerous degree in that the subjective feelings are the basis for serving rather than an objective, ideological commitment to doing the work of Christ in the world, bringing people to the Saviour, and being obedient.

Yaconelli and Burns again speak to this issue in *High School Ministry:* "Making a first commitment to Christ at camp [or through a missions project, for that matter] is a wonderful experience, but then comes the work—living that commitment when we don't feel like it. We must always live with the tension of balancing experiential truth with propositional truth."[10]

Observation #7—Students Are Frustrated

Being a teenager is not easy, and it seems to get more difficult with time. Choices are open to students at younger and younger ages, with greater and greater intensity, and less and less emphasis on generally acceptable norms and values. In 1950, a student faced the choice of preserving his or her virginity; in 1990, a student must decide between heterosexual, homosexual, or bisexual "options." In 1960, a high schooler might have gotten drunk or even experimented with marijuana; in 1990, a junior higher has peers who are alcoholics and has access to life-threatening cocaine.

Students get frustrated and angry because they need help in this myriad of choices, and they do not know where to turn. In addition, they are progressively becoming frustrated with their own experiences in life. What they have been led to expect about life is simply not occurring.

In an article in *Pastoral Renewal*, youth observer Michael Keating summarized the frustration in young people, especially as it is related to the media:

> Because the media-created world is so forceful and pervasive, the youth believe in it, even when it does not square

with their own experience. "There's a big party going on, and everyone's having a good time—it's just me who's out of it. Promiscuous sex and drinking bouts are liberating and fun—it's just me who's miserable and can't get them to work right. The world is full of beautiful and sexy people with no problems—it's just me who's ugly and a loser."[11]

Our Response

To these youth of our times we come. They may be selfish, confused, frustrated, and rebellious—but are any of these tendencies new? Indeed, the intensity of the challenges we face may be new, but the issues are still very basic to human nature. We must not set up a mental barrier in our work with youth that causes us to view them as some bizarre breed of animal.

Instead, we should do our best to know young people and the world out of which they come so that we can respond accordingly. With a specific mindset for missions involvement and the growth related to this, we must still make some basic responses in all of our youth work which will be the foundation for all that is done related to missions.

Response #1—Take Teenagers Seriously

A fellow youth worker once received one of our high school mailings; in response to it, he commented on my reference at the beginning of the letter, "Dear high school men and women."

"How come you refer to your students as *men* and *women*?" he asked.

"Because I believe young people respond to the way we treat them. If we give them respect and honor as adults, I believe they will be more inclined to behave that way. On the other hand, if we see them only as 'kids,' they will behave according to our expectations."

Teenagers are, in the words of one writer, "passionately desiring to be taken seriously."[12] Their retreat to peer friendships as their only trusted companions, their frustration, and even their hopelessness toward the future is—in some respects—related to the fact that the adult world does not take them seriously. Their concerns, priorities, questions and needs are not respected by the world of "grown-ups."

Ronald Kotesky, in his fine book *Understanding Adolescence*, repeatedly makes the point that the basic thing that parents can do to communicate more effectively with their teenagers is "to treat them as much like adults as possible."[13] He goes on to add that "your expectations as parents are probably the most important factors in your teenagers acting like adults."[14] In other words, if we treat them like adults, they are more inclined to respond as adults.

Neither Ronald Kotesky or I are suggesting that teenagers should be hurried into adult life, a problem addressed by David Elkind in his book, *All Grown Up and No Place to Go*.[15] Instead, we are saying that teenagers should be listened to, taken seriously, and challenged to live up to their full potential.

In a seminar with youth leaders, I was explaining the current needs of the young people in our youth ministry. One of the participants approached me after the seminar with a personal question. He asked, "Where did you get that list of needs that you cited?"

I know this man was expecting me to refer to some new book, survey, or newsletter. He was amazed, however, when I gave my simple response: "I asked the students I work with."

"What a great idea," he replied. "I never thought of that."

We need to make use of anything we can read or study to help us understand young people, but we are wise to *listen to them*, take their responses and perceptions seriously, and then try to respond.

Response #2—Help Them Integrate

Teenagers separate faith and daily living. How come? Perhaps because their parents and the older Christian examples they have before them fail to integrate faith and life. Indeed, all of us are hypocrites—talking about Christian faith in ways that we are unable to live it. No wonder that teenagers follow us.

In spite of the challenge, however, youth leaders must make aggressive overtures toward integration. In the words of Yaconelli and Burns again, "We must help students relate their faith to every other area of their lives, not by making them feel guilty, but by helping them realize that faith in Christ affects all of life. We must teach our young people that faith is not merely one of the things we do in life, it is the basis of *all* that we do."[16]

To help students integrate faith, we need activity-oriented learning as well as cognitive input, but more than anything else, we and other leaders must try to exemplify integrated lives. Our lives must be marked by a personal faith that is related to our daily living. The need for good examples is one full section of this book because teenagers—like adults—are looking for models to emulate.

Response #3—Don't Underestimate Teenagers

In pursuing titles related to youth work, I came across one that caught my eye: *Giving Youth a Better Chance.* The title itself responds to the negativism that is often associated with adolescents. Too often we—both in the church and in our culture at large— assume the worst about teenagers, and we fail to give them the opportunities they need to grow and thrive.

In *Understanding Adolescence,* Ronald Kotesky refers to the first major work done on adolescence in 1904—*Sturm and Drang*— Storm and Stress.[17] Since that time, numerous works have been written about teenagers, and many refer only to the negative aspects of the adolescent years—*Parents in Pain,*[18] *Growing Pains,*[19] or even *Five Cries of Youth.*[20] While all of these titles accurately reflect the tumult that often accompanies the youth years, they can easily cause youth leaders and parents to assume the worst about teenagers and preteens.

We need to consider "giving youth a better chance." We need more titles like *You Can Make a Difference,*[21] or *Let's Succeed with Our Teenagers.*[22] If we start with a negative posture, we may be guilty of assuming the worst. This book is written from a more positive approach because—in my years of youth ministry experience—I have found that teenagers are full of potential. They surely do carry with them many stresses and strains related to adolescence, puberty, family breakdown, and negative self-esteem, but giving them the opportunity to succeed, to lead, to "make a difference," is the best way that we have found to help them rise above their circumstances.

Response #4—Show Them How to Make a Difference

The potential of young people will go untapped if we do not give them opportunities to make a difference in the world. I became acutely aware of the frustration we can cause in young people when I presented challenges without practical responses in a youth meeting several years ago. I talked about world needs—1 billion hungry, 2 billion without knowledge of Christ, 16,000 unreached people groups.

After the meeting, one student approached me and blurted out his frustration. *"What do you want me to do?"* he exclaimed. "I am only one person!"

What can one person do? If we believe that each one *can* make a difference, we must show them how—in practical, realistic ways. In *Giving Youth a Better Chance,* the author concludes with various suggestions for implementation, including giving students more opportunities for service:

> The period of dependence and lack of involvement of young people in society's problems has become more prolonged, even while the gradual reduction of the age of puberty has meant earlier maturity. Young people need "a piece of the action." Largely as a result of extensive exposure to TV, they tend to know more about social problems than did earlier generations, but they have little opportunity to do anything about them.[23]

An effective response to young people—who might otherwise grow frustrated and pessimistic about their role in society—is to let them serve. "Service is a step away from the sense of entitlement that is so widespread today. Service places the emphasis on responsibility to others and on *active participation in society"* (author's emphasis).[24] We must show young people how they can make a difference in our world.

Response #5—Give Youth a Place of Belonging

The need and desire for close, intimate friendship should be easily addressed in the Christian youth group. This need is often associated with terms like "body of Christ," "God's family," or even "fellowship."

The problem, however, is that—without active commitment to the group (or the church)—youth seldom feel that they really belong. They may feel entertained, taught, or even ministered to, but they may also feel useless and unnecessary. Only with involvement do they feel that they belong to each other, to the church, and even to God.

How can this happen? Youth group projects, teamwork, and active involvement in the church are themes that will emerge throughout the book. All of our efforts at missions, service, and growth will be in vain if we do not take into account the fact that friendship and a sense of belonging are primary motivators in the young people we serve.

Response #6—Tell Students the Truth

In our efforts to attract students to Christian commitment or to missions involvement, we will find ourselves prone to exaggerate the benefits of service over the hardships. This may lead to greater short-term results but also more long-term disillusionment and student fall-out.

We need to tell them the truth. Christianity does not provide easy answers. Hardship is part of following Christ. "What works"— in other words, the pragmatic solution—might not be the Christian answer.

The same is true in service. Although serving others will lead to greater long-term growth and Christlikeness (the basic premise of this book), it may not be *fun*.

In our efforts to help students integrate faith and life, and in our responses to their aversion for the ideological, we need to realize that they must hear the truth. If we do not associate Christian faith with truth, honest responses, and discernment, then we make Christianity no more believable than television. Listen to the evaluation of Arthur Levine:

> Television has failed. Television is the greatest educational experiment ever attempted. Increasingly, it performs roles once filled by the family, the schools, and the church. But television does not provide liberal education. In fact, it lies. During the past three decades, television has provided America with a distorted image of itself, alternating the idealized and the sordid. It has minimized the contribution of women, minorities, the aged, and the handicapped to our society. It has exalted violence and enshrined commercial values. For all problems there is a product, and for every product there is a problem that is solved. Instead of educating the young, television has sold them products, junk food as well as drugs, and socialized them for a consumer society. It has fostered in the young a jaundiced and more fearful view of the society than is warranted.[25]

In the preparation of our summer outreach teams, we often confront truth versus falsehood in the expectations of our students.

They learn that growth often comes more through hardship, that prayer is easier in the face of crisis, that service is a form of dying (see John 12:24). In all of our presentations, we look with hope to the fact that God is in control, that He brings good out of difficulty, but truthfulness requires us to acknowledge that it is not going to be easy.

One of our summer teams required the reading of *Lords of the Earth*[26] by Don Richardson as part of their team preparation. A team member approached me after reading the book. She was quite upset.

"That was a *horrible* book," she said.

"Why?" I responded. "Wasn't it a story of a man mightily used by God?"

"Yes," she agreed.

"And wasn't it a powerful testimony of the Gospel at work to overcome sin?" I continued.

She agreed again.

"And wasn't it a great missionary story?" I asked again.

"Yes, but . . ."

"But what?" I asked.

"But before the tribe believes the Gospel, they kill the missionary, cut him into little pieces, and scatter him all over the jungle." She identified her problem.

"And you don't like it that the guy did good and still got killed?" I continued.

"Yes," she said, "I guess that's it."

"Well, I said, "think about what happened to Jesus. Sometimes obedience to God brings greater hardship, at least in this life, but we find peace in the fact that God does bring good out of hardship in the end—even when we don't see it."

"I guess you're right," she concluded, "but that doesn't make it easier."

Tell them the truth.

The young people of our age offer their own unique challenges, but their potential can still be tapped by appropriate responses and by giving them the opportunities to make a difference.

Ernest Becker is said to have stated, "Youth was not made for pleasure, but for heroism." If we seek to understand young people, respond to their needs, and then involve them in being "heroes," we shall indeed raise up a generation with broader world views and a greater confidence in God that they can reach out and become world-changers.

NOTES

[1]*Youthworker Update* is published monthly by Youth Specialties Ministries, 1224 Greenfield Dr., El Cajon, CA 92021.

[2]Don Posterski, *Friendship: A Window on Ministry to Youth* (Scarborough, Ontario: Project Teen Canada, 1985).

[3]Don Posterski, "Profile of the Emerging Generation" (handout prepared for workshop leaders at the Urbana '87 Missions Convention by Inter-Varsity Christian Fellowship), p. 1.

[4]*Real Friends* is the title of Barbara Varenhorst's book on peer counseling (San Francisco: Harper and Row, 1983).

[5]Arthur Levine, *When Dreams and Heroes Died* (San Francisco: Jossey-Bass, 1980), p. 122.

[6]*Tension Getters I and II* are published by Zondervan/Youth Specialties, and they focus on a case-study approach which gets students discussing hypothetical issues related to family, school, moral choices, and ethical dilemmas. They are very helpful in discovering what students *really* believe.

[7]Mike Yaconelli and Jim Burns, *High School Ministry* (Grand Rapids: Zondervan, 1987), p. 65.

[8]This is especially emphasized in the book by Susan Littwin, *The Postponed Generation* (New York: William Morrow and Co., 1986).

[9]Posterski, "Profile of the Emerging Generation," p. 1.

[10]Yaconelli and Burns, *High School Ministry*, p. 65.

[11]Michael Keating, "Highway to Hell" (*Pastoral Renewal*, June 1987), p. 4.

[12]Michael Keating, "The Stolen Generation" (*Pastoral Renewal*, May 1987), p. 12.

[13]Ronald L. Kotesky, *Understanding Adolescence* (Wheaton, Illinois: Victor Books, 1987), pp. 20, 32.

[14]*Ibid.*, p. 21.

[15]David Elkind, *All Grown Up and No Place to Go* (Reading, Massachusetts: Addison-Wesley, 1984).

[16]Yaconelli and Burns, *High School Ministry*, p. 65.

[17]Kotesky, *op. cit.*, p. 17.

[18]John White, *Parents in Pain* (Downers Grove, Illinois: InterVarsity Press, 1979).

[19]Fred Hartley, *Growing Pains* (Old Tappan, New Jersey: Fleming Revell, 1981).

[20]Merton P. Strommen, *Five Cries of Youth* (New York: Harper and Row, 1974).

[21]Tony Campolo, *You Can Make a Difference!* (Waco, Texas: Word, 1984).

[22]Jay Kesler, *Let's Succeed with Our Teenagers* (Elgin, Illinois: David C. Cook, 1973).

[23]Carnegie Council on Policy Studies in Higher Education, *Giving Youth a Better Chance*

(San Francisco: Jossey-Bass, 1979), pp. 269–270.

[24]Levine, *Dreams and Heroes*, p. 137.

[25]Levine, *Dreams and Heroes*, pp. 135–36.

[26]Don Richards, *Lords of the Earth* (Glendale, California: Regal, 1985).

CHAPTER TWO
MOTIVATING YOUTH
TOWARD WORLD MISSIONS

If our goal is to expand the world views of the young people with whom we work, we start by knowing and responding to them and their basic needs and perceptions (chapter 1). This is basic to all effective youth work.

If we desire to go further, however, and touch their priorities in such a way that they will graduate our youth ministries with a desire to help change the world, we must realize that we are up against a greater challenge. We are presenting to them a Christianity that goes counter to our culture—even counter to some aspects of the "Christian culture."

Karl Marx, the cofounder of the Communist movement, wrote with Friedrich Engels a book entitled *The Communist Manifesto*. It was the platform on which Communism was built and a work by which every modern person is affected.

In this work of 1847, Marx and Engels challenged the world with their thoughts: "Let the ruling classes tremble at a communist revolution. The proletarians have nothing to lose but their chains. They have a world to win."

With these words, Marx and Engels began a movement (with goals of world "conquest") that affects the entire population of the world today. They may have been deluded, misguided, and atheistic, but they had a dream, a vision to which they recruited others and for which they expended their lives.

Do we have such a vision of the coming of God's Kingdom? Are we as consumed by the desire to see Christ proclaimed in the earth as Marx was to liberate the proletariat? We too perceive our goal as a "world to win." Will we give ourselves to the cause?

What Are We After?

When we speak of "expanding our youth group's world view," what do we mean? Does it mean that the students in the group become geography experts? Will it mean success in discussions of international politics? What will it mean?

There are three basic goals at which we can aim as we set ourselves to doing our part in channeling youth toward the world we have to win.

Goal #1—To Produce "World Christians"

The phrase "world Christians" has been popularized in missions discussions, and we are wise to make use of it. David Bryant, in the book *In the Gap*, uses it widely. His definition gives us an excellent starting point:

> World Christians are day-to-day disciples for whom Christ's global cause has become the integrating overriding priority for all that He is for them. Like disciples should, they actively investigate all that their Master's Great Commission means. Then they act on what they learn. [1]

Missiologist J. Herbert Kane defines a "world Christian" this way: "As a child of the kingdom the believer then becomes a world Christian. By calling he belongs to a universal fellowship—the Christian church. By conviction he proclaims a universal message—the Christian Gospel. By commitment he owes his allegiance to a universal king—Jesus Christ. By vocation, he is part of a universal movement—the Christian mission." [2]

The youth leader's challenge is to produce young people who are thinking about a world beyond themselves. To be a teenage "world Christian" is to be uncharacteristically unselfish with time, service, money, and prayer. It will mean a concern for people who do not know Christ and a willingness to go beyond the secure peer group into the "unknown" of outreach.

Goal #2—To Produce Servants

Involving youth in world missions is not just an exercise in expanding their international viewpoints. It is to stir them to see the need for servants in our world today and to challenge them to be those servants.

The 1980 Conference on World Evangelism in Pattaya, Thailand called for 200,000 new missionaries by the year 2000. Where are these servants going to come from?

While many will go from the Third World into other parts of the world, there is still a great need for those to go from the West—including across cultural barriers here in the United States! Where will these servants come from? Our youth groups are excellent sources!

Our desire in youth missions is to help broaden a student's perspective enough so that he or she considers missionary service as *a normal result* of Christian obedience. Too many students graduate high school thinking that missionaries come from one of two groups—either the "supersaints" or the "losers" (who had to go somewhere else because they were useless here in their own country). If we want to correct those misconceptions, we start by showing our students where they might fit into God's global plan, and that God may want to use them as missionaries.

Producing servants is, again, countercultural. As one Third-World leader stated, "The total self-absorption of Americans in their own self-examination has, in a sense, increased the insensitivity with which the United States now looks at the world."[4] Our young people grow up in this world and, if they do not develop a servant-orientation (which will counteract that insensitivity) through our youth groups and churches, they will perpetuate the selfishness.

Goal #3—To Produce World-changers

We have a world to win, and together with the young people that God has put in our care we can do our part. But such action means a reorientation of their priorities and ours. Rather than selfishness, we will need to be servants. Rather than pessimism, we must focus on possibilities for change. Rather than a cloistered self-concern, we will need to reach out.

The writers of *Campus Life* magazine addressed this need to be "world-changers" in an article entitled "Using Life."[5] They tell the stories of young people who chose to leave behind their dreams of megabucks for lives of service and sacrifice. They confront their readers with choices we need to put before our students (and ourselves) with regularity:

> With the one life you have, you could go for money, success, power. Most people do. Others choose to forget the American Dream to become *revolutionaries in a different cause* (author's emphasis).[6]

Earlier we observed that a good youth ministry response to today's teenager was to tell them the truth—be honest. If we sincerely hope that they will be world-changers, we must let them know that there is sacrifice involved. Unfortunately, in our affluence, we (unlike Marx's proletariat) have much more to lose than our chains. We have dreams, comforts, pleasures, and possessions. As we face the sacrifice of these for the cause of Christ, our priorities will be put to the test.

The writers of the resource notebook *How to Organize a Mission Program in the Local Church* spell out the challenge of producing "world-changers" quite succinctly:

> Teenagers must be challenged by the Great Commission of Jesus Christ—challenged to dedicate themselves to the fulfillment of Christ's mission on earth. They must be helped to understand the church's program in missions throughout the world. They must be helped to understand the political and social powers at work on the fields and against which the Christian Gospel is struggling. They must be given the chance to help solve the problems of repression, ignorance, and superstition that they might help the downtrodden to find opportunity to find life, fulfillment, and redemption in Christ.[7]

Quoting again from Marx: "Philosophers and historians have only interpreted the world. The point, however, is to change it." Indeed, this is our goal by the power of the Gospel, and to this end we can challenge our youth.

How Do We Do It?

The goals—world Christians, servants, world-changers—are noble-sounding, but how do we get there? Most of us in youth ministry spend our time with more mundane questions: "Where's the volleyball pump?" "Who's taking registrations for the retreat?" "What will we study in Sunday School?" "When's the next parents' meeting?"

Talking of young people as "world-changers" sounds strange to the youth worker who has just struggled through an all-nighter with 20 junior high boys. He might see their potential as world "rearrangers" but world Christian servants?

Indeed, the basic concepts of this book are built on a *long-term view* of youth ministry. I have had the opportunity to see youth group alumni go out in missionary service at great personal sacrifice and cost. But I can remember these same people being disruptive in Sunday School, making out with their girlfriends on the bus, and causing a general nuisance for their parents. I can testify that the missionaries of the future are not always the ideal youth group members of the present.

Nevertheless, there are some choices of perspective that we can make in helping teenagers grow to their full potential as world-changers (and be strengthened ourselves in the process).

Perspective #1—Growth Takes Time

The reader could inaccurately assume that our youth/missions program at Grace Chapel is nothing but a string of unending successes. How false! We have sent out mission teams that have done the wrong work, experienced relational upheaval, and even had a negative influence on students regarding world missions. Some of our fund-raisers have been total flops and others never got off the ground because we could not muster student interest or parental support.

In spite of all of the failures, however, we have seen many graduate from our youth ministry with a changed perspective on the world and their roles in it. Some are on the mission field, while others are preparing to be missionary doctors, "tentmaker" missionaries in limited-access countries, or even missions-minded pastors and lay leaders. Over the course of many years, the reminder that "growth takes time" has been a great comfort, because the results in the lives of students (or in my own life, for that matter) are seldom as rapid as I would like.

Perspective #2—The Value of the Individual

Seeing people as God does is a tremendous challenge for youth workers. Terms like "potential" and "resources for Christ's kingdom" are hard to apply to teenagers whom we sometimes see as arrogant, selfish, misbehaved, or rebellious. The truth remains (regardless of how unlikely it may seem to us) that God loves these young people and will delight in using their energies for His Kingdom.

Dr. Tony Campolo speaks to this theme repeatedly in his book (and the film series) *You Can Make a Difference!* The story of Billy, the kid with cerebral palsy and a host of other birth defects is an

inspiration. At junior high camp, Billy was being repeatedly ma-
ligned and abused by fellow campers. Dr. Campolo tells the rest of
the story:

> The level of meanness reached its lowest point on a
> Wednesday morning. Billy's cabin had been assigned the
> morning devotions for that camp of 150 kids. All of the
> boys in his cabin had voted for Billy to be the speaker. I
> knew, and they knew that he couldn't do it; they just
> wanted to get him up there so that they could mock him
> and laugh. They thought it would be fun to watch "spastic
> Billy" try to deliver a devotional talk. I was irate. And I
> was livid. I was seething with anger as little Billy got up
> out of his seat and limped his way to the platform. You
> could hear the titters of mocking laughter and sneering
> going through the group. I could not remember ever be-
> ing so angry. What was amazing was that the ridicule of
> the boys didn't stop that little guy. He took his place on
> the rostrum and started to speak. It took Billy almost ten
> tortured minutes to say, "Je-sus loves meee! Je-Je-Je-sus
> loves meee! Annd-I-I-love Je-Je-Jesus." And when he fin-
> ished there was dead silence. I looked over my shoulder,
> and there were junior high school boys shaking and trem-
> bling and crying all over the place.
>
> A revival broke out in that camp and kids turned their
> lives over to Jesus. A host of junior high boys committed
> their lives to Christian service. I wish I had kept count of
> how many ministers I have met as I travel across this
> country who have told me that they gave their lives to
> Jesus because of the witness of a "spastic" kid named
> Billy.[8]

Whenever I am tempted to give up on a student for any number
of reasons, I remember this story of Billy, and I remember that
"Redeemer" is one of the powerful names associated with our
Saviour.

Perspective #3—The Mustard Seed Principle

Like many other youth workers, I have wondered occasionally,
"Why am I doing this? I should have gone into business." The
efforts, programs, relationships, and problems can be overwhelming

at times, especially if we see few results.

The "mustard seed" principle can help revive us. It is the basic belief that God can take the smallest thing (in Jesus' example, a mustard seed) and turn it into something mighty. When we first started the summer mission team program at Grace Chapel, there were many problems and a fair amount of opposition. I never knew then that later in my life I would be helping others to do the same through seminars or books. All I knew was that "youth and missions" was having a hard time getting off the ground. Today I look back and see the mustard seed principle at work: God took our tiny efforts and turned them into something mighty for His kingdom.

Tony Campolo again shares a mustard seed story of his involvement with several students confronting a multinational corporation in the Dominican Republic:

> We accused them of growing sugar on land which would be better used to grow food for the hungry Dominicans. We condemned them for not being responsive to the needs of the Dominican people, claiming that they did not provide adequate housing and services for the thousands of workers they employed. We showed up at the stockholders meetings of the corporation and supported resolutions condemning company practices. In all of these condemnations and efforts we accomplished nothing. Eventually we abandoned these tactics realizing that the corporation was far too powerful to be intimidated by a few crusaders who held a few shares of stock. Little by little we ended our confrontational strategy and entered into a cooperative relationship. The leaders of the corporation surprised us. What we could never have forced them to do, they did willingly. They committed $100 million to the social and economic development of the Dominican Republic. The company is building schools, developing medical programs, constructing homes for their workers, and making land that formerly grew sugar available to grow crops for indigenous consumption.[9]

God took their mustard seed efforts, transformed them in the process (from confronters to cooperators), and turned their efforts into a mighty impact for good. Keeping the view that God will increase our efforts in His time will help us endure the hard times of wondering if it is really worth it.

Perspective #4—The History of Modern Missions

I am not much of a historian, but I do know that young people have been integrally important in the advance of the Gospel worldwide over the past 250 years. This is the message of David Howard in his book *Student Power in World Missions:*

> When students decide to act, things happen. That's the history of missions. For the missionary movement has had a tremendous vitality often sparked by students with a worldwide vision.[10]

From the Haystack Prayer Meeting to the Student Volunteer Movement; from William Carey to Hudson Taylor to Jim Elliot; from Youth with a Mission to Operation Mobilization; from the great Urbana Missions Conferences to Teen Missions International to our youth groups . . . God has and will raise up young people with a vision for evangelizing the world which can affect the entire church and renew a much-needed zeal for the completion of Christ's global commission.

The great missionary to Japan and China, Francis Xavier, is said to have bemoaned the apathy he heard of among students in his native France. He wanted to return and run up and down the streets of Paris telling students to "give up their small ambitions and come eastward to preach the Gospel of Christ."

We ourselves may bemoan apathy, the size of the worldwide task, or even the challenge of sensitizing students to needs beyond themselves, but if we desire to motivate them to make a difference in our world, we too must "give up our small ambitions" and draw on God's strength to rise to the tasks before us.

NOTES
[1]David Bryant, *In the Gap* (Ventura, California: Regal, 1985), p. 93.

[2]J. Herbert Kane, *Wanted: World Christians!* (Grand Rapids, Michigan: Baker, 1986) pp. 137–138.

[3]*Ibid.*

[4]From a speech by Soedjatmoko (former Indonesian ambassador to the United States), "Is America Listening to Asia?" *International Educational and Cultural Exchange* (Winter 1977), p. 5.

[5]Chris Lutes, "Using Life," *Campus Life* (January 1986), p. 42.

[6]*Ibid.*

[7]"Education for Missions," *How to Organize a Missions Program in the Local Church* (Ivyland, Pennsylvania: Neibauer Press, 1973), p. 47.

[8]Tony Campolo, *You Can Make a Difference* (Waco, Texas: Word, 1984), pp. 48–49.

[9]Tony Campolo, *Ideas for Social Action* (Grand Rapids, Michigan: Zondervan/Youth Specialties, 1984), p. 19.

[10]David Howard, *Student Power in World Missions* (Downers Grove, Illinois: InterVarsity Press, 1979), back cover.

EXPANDING YOUR STUDENTS' WORLD VIEW
Basic Ingredient #1—EXAMPLES

Today's young people are pessimistic, nonintegrated, and pragmatic. But beyond any of these other possible negative characteristics, young people are a product of our age. Very few of these negative tendencies were created by the teenagers alone; they learned these and a variety of other negative viewpoints from us.

The response and remedy to these problems also lie with us. Effective models of leadership and servanthood are the most powerful tools to change the lives and perspectives of the young people with whom we work. More than anything else, they need to see examples of *lives well lived*. They are looking for models to follow, and we can provide them.

The need for effective examples is nowhere more mandatory than in the realm of expanding one's view of the world. If we hope to stimulate young people to be world Christians, we need to make sure that the older people who are influencing young people are likewise world Christians.

The educators from the Association of Church Missions Committees write:

> Youth are looking for a life to emulate. Youth leaders, teachers, parents, pastors, Christian nationals, and missionaries need to present integrated, authentic, consistent lives as world Christians for youth to emulate.[1]

Missions expert David Bryant carries the topic of integration even further when he writes, "More and more I am convinced that we really must help missions-minded people to *integrate* a vision for the world into every facet of their walk with Christ."[2]

As Jesus said to his disciples, and as Paul said to his, we need to say to the young people of our ministries, "Follow me."[3] "*Nothing* motivates students more than a real model."[4]

I have sometimes wondered why students will endure the grease and frustration of working their first jobs at the McDonald's fast-food chain. An article in *Reader's Digest* gave me an insight into the strategic impact of good modeling. The chairman of the board—who started out as a grill worker in 1956–is still expected to "roll up his sleeves and pitch in, doing what has made McDonald's famous."[5] The chief executive officer helps out at some of the 200 restaurants he visits each year, often "taking orders and passing out Big Macs."[6]

"Follow me." This is the power of a good example, and if we desire to assist our students as they grow to have broadened world visions, we must start by providing these examples.

NOTES

[1]From the *Missions Education Handbook* (Wheaton, Illinois: Association of Church Missions Committees, 1981), p. 47.

[2]Personal correspondence with David Bryant, December 7, 1987.

[3]See Matthew 4:19 and 1 Corinthians 11:1.

[4]Dave Busby, "Creating a Willingness within Students for Spiritual Maturity," *Discipling the Young Person* (Arrowhead Springs, California: Here's Life, 1985), p. 166.

[5]Per Ola and Emil d'Aulaire, "60 Billion Burgers and Counting," *Reader's Digest* (December 1987), p. 44.

[6]*Ibid.*

CHAPTER THREE
THE EXAMPLE OF CHURCH LEADERS AND PASTORS

My own missions interest and commitment is a result of missions-minded church leaders and pastors. From my earliest days of commitment to Christ, I can recall a zeal for world missions from our senior pastor and the ruling lay boards. This example in our leadership has been continued over many years, and the impact is still powerfully felt among the young people.

Although the senior pastor does not always have a lot of direct contact with the high school students, his example may still be the most profound. Praying regularly for the missionaries supported by the church can reinforce his stated commitment to support those who go out. Perhaps the pastor will address subjects related to world events or pray for crises on the international front: both speak of a world awareness.

On the personal level, a word of affirmation to missions-interested students or even a note of encouragement can go a long way. Some students might be affected by a visit to the pastor's office, especially if there is a prominent world map or a poster board of missionary pictures from around the world.

Church leaders can have a similar effect on students by their affirmation and their prayers. Our missions elder, Dan, will regularly get some names from me of missions-minded young people, and then he will find them at church and tell them that he is praying for them. The conversation may not last long, but it sends a signal to the student that the church is behind him or her.

One of the most potent examples from our church leaders has been their own willingness to go overseas themselves. When pastoral staff members travel to visit missionaries or participate on a work team, they send the loud message: "I am not asking you to do anything that I myself am not willing to do."

Our lay leaders have carried out an exemplary role with our young people by committing themselves to serve in cross-cultural ministries. Some have made mid-career changes while others have taken early retirement so as to go out in missionary service. These adult examples trickle down to create a missions enthusiasm that affects the youth group.

What If My Pastor Is Not Missions-minded?

In most churches, the preaching pastor is still the most influential person in determining the overall direction and priorities of the church. What if he or she is not missions-minded? What can a world-minded youth leader do?

We start by assuming the best about our pastor. Perhaps there is a commitment to missions present, but the daily demands of ministry and the expectations of others divert his attention. If this is true, we can assist our pastors by feeding them information about missions and missionaries.

Many churches are trying to build their pastors' mission interest by sending them overseas to visit missionaries. This can be a tremendous asset to the church-missions vision if it is a "planned success" for the pastor. (The goal of a cross-cultural ministry is to build the pastor's vision—not destroy it. A visit to some Third-World city or to a refugee camp in southeast Asia might not be the place to start with a pastor who has never been outside the United States. If the experience is so harsh or overwhelming that the pastor is stunned, he may retreat from talking about missions at all and return to the safety of his own little world.) A "planned success" gives the pastor cross-cultural experiences in gradual dosages so that he returns excited about the cross-cultural ministry and desirous of returning.

Other ideas for expanding your pastor's world vision might be:

• Involve him in projects the youth group is doing.

• Encourage him to preach on missions or missions-related themes.

• Send him to one of the Urbana Missions Conferences[1] or to the ACMC National Conference.[2]

• Get him on a few mission organizations' mailing lists.

• Encourage him to pray for one missionary need per week in the pastoral prayer.

• Take him out for international food. (I was once with seven pastors who were asking me how to build an excitement for missions in their churches. We went out to lunch at a Mexican restaurant, and I discovered that six had never eaten Mexican food before. I told them that excitement about missions might start right there at lunch, because they were starting to experience a little about another culture.)

• Buy him a map or a world globe.

Most of these ideas will not be the responsibility of the youth leaders but rather of the missions committee. If there is no missions committee, however, youth leaders are wise to use these ideas so that the church grows in its vision for the world. It is difficult to expand the world view of students under a pastor who does not care about missions and the world beyond his church's normal reach.

What about Church Leaders?

Some of the ideas above are useful, especially membership in the Association of Church Missions Committees. The best thing that youth leaders can do to encourage good "world Christian" modeling on behalf of church leaders is to remind them of the powerful impact that they have on the whole church.

One traditional poem starts off, "I'd rather *see a sermon* than hear one any day. . . ." If our young people are to develop expanded world views, they can be greatly encourged if they are following the example of pastors and church leaders who are setting the pace.

NOTES

[1]Offered every three years by Inter-Varsity Christian Fellowship, P.O. Box 7895, Madison, Wisconsin 53707.

[2]There are two annual conferences; contact the Association of Church Missions Committees, P.O. Box ACMC, Wheaton, Illinois 60189.

CHAPTER FOUR
THE EXAMPLE OF YOUTH LEADERS

Those people with the best opportunity to illustrate concern for world missions are the youth leaders, sponsors, and lay leaders who work with the youth. Though youth leaders can follow in the same tracks as the pastor by their prayers, maps, affirmation, and travels, the greatest asset that youth leaders have is their own willingness to consider missionary service for themselves.

Young people are sensitive to hypocrisy. If they approach a youth leader with the question, "If you are so concerned about missions, how come you are not a missionary?" the youth leader must have a good response. If the only response is an uncomfortable hemming and hawing, the youth may see the leader as a hypocrite.

Bob Pierce, the founder of World Vision International, addressed this need for the youth leader's example in his book *Emphasizing Missions in the Local Church:*

> A personal obedience to the missionary vision is a primary requisite for the young people's sponsor if he would instill this vision in the hearts and minds of those under his guidance.[1]

Pastor E.G. Von Trutschler is one of the most potent illustrations of the youth leader's power through example. Listen first to his underlying philosophy:

> E.G. Von Trutschler (Pastor "Von") of San Diego, an experienced youth worker who has taken hundreds of young people into Mexico and South America to serve the poor, says this: "I would never think of leading kids somewhere I've never been. No way. It destroys your credibility. You need more than words. You've got to be able to say to kids, 'Here's what we're going to do, and I'll show you how.' You can't be a leader the first time. You will need to

go first, analyze the territory, get to know the people, find out what needs to be done, and then say to the kids, 'Follow me.' There may be times when the leaders will have to learn the ropes right along with the kids, but it is generally true that your leaders will be more effective if they can lead from their own experience."[2]

Without people to back up his theories, however, Pastor Von could be just another youth ministry philosopher, but his life speaks loudly to verify his ideas. For over twenty years, Von has been leading young people into Mexico and South America, showing them how to do cross-cultural, caring ministry. Von has nurtured dozens of young people who serve in a broad variety of ministries and missions.[3]

Rick Johnson is one of those students. He now heads a ministry called International Youth Missions, an organization dedicated to getting young people into "authentic discipleship" opportunities, especially in Mexico.

In an interview in *Youthworker Journal*, Rick expressed some very strong ideas about the need for good youth leader modeling and the impact on the students (and the size of the ministry):

> *YJ:* What would you tell the youth worker who's trying to move his kids in this direction, but finds that they aren't interested?
>
> *JOHNSON:* I honestly haven't run into very many youth workers like that. Kids know that something's missing in their faith, but they don't know what it is. They look at their youth leaders and they don't find role models. We've found over and over through our Mexican ministry that kids get turned on when they have an opportunity to express their love for Christ. They find the "something" that was missing in their Christian lives.
>
> The problem for youth workers is that if they commit to a more authentic discipling ministry, they'll have smaller groups, at least at first. Our numbers will drop. We aren't going to have many kids who will go to an old folks' home and wipe the barf off of some retarded man's face or sit and listen to some woman talk for hours on end about her problems. But if our churches understand that we're not just going for numbers, that we're going for quality, we

can survive the transition. I've seen one hundred kids in a youth group that tomorrow will be one hundred worthless adults. What's the value in that?

What we youth workers have to give up to make this kind of discipleship work is our need to be successful in the world's eyes. We all want to have big youth groups. It may be, though, that God has other things on His mind.[4]

Tough words—but these are words we need to hear because they speak to the challenge that we face ourselves as followers of Christ. Am I willing to follow Christ in service into the world if it means that my youth ministry looks like a failure—at least in the world's eyes (but maybe in my church's too?). Am *I* willing to listen for hours to some old woman's problems or "wipe the barf off some retarded man's face"?

Perhaps the reason that more youth groups are not missions-oriented has more to do with us youth leaders than with the selfishness of our students.

In thinking through our role as examples before our students, we may start to wonder how this exemplary role will demonstrate itself in our lives. Consider five specific ways that we youth leaders should lead the way toward greater Christlikeness and the missions-mindedness that follows.

Example #1—Obedience

Several years ago, a student actually did approach me with this question: "If you are so hot about this missions stuff, why aren't you a missionary?"

Fortunately, I had an answer. My wife and I had just returned from an Urbana conference where we opened our lives to the Lord for whatever He wanted for us as husband and wife. God directed us quite clearly to stay put and to continue in our efforts to influence others, but the conversation with that student taught us a lesson. We need to be pacesetters in obedience to the call of the Lord of the harvest.

As a result, my wife and I take time out every three to four years to evaluate God's call again. Rather than choosing the easy or the comfortable just because it is here in front of us, we recognize our own need to resubmit ourselves with regularity to the Lord for possible reassignment. By doing this, we feel more capable of asking students to do the same.

Example #2—Servanthood

I have traveled with Von Trutschler into Mexico, and I have seen him in action. There is no job too mundane, no responsibility too dirty for him to undertake. He leads others into servanthood by serving.

There is the example that Jesus provided the 12 disciples in John 13, exemplifying servanthood by serving. It is the same example we must show before our students.

A few years ago, our senior pastor developed a new motto for us on staff. He told us that we should all be trying at all times to be "first-performers." By this, he meant that we should seek to lead our people by example, performing first at even the most insignificant tasks. This is servant leadership—making sure that our lives exemplify the type of sacrificial servanthood that we want to produce.

Example #3—Faith

Whenever we get into serving beyond our own secure worlds, it will involve risk, and risk means faith. Being good examples to our students means that we step out in faith just as we are asking them to do.

In the first summer of our summer teams, the major obstacle for our students was the cost. When students asked me about it, I told them that they needed to trust God with their needs.

Little did I know that I would find myself in need of $1,000 for the summer's activities. I decided that I had to follow my own advice and trust God. Over the next few weeks, checks came in for $400, $300, and $200. With ten days left before the deadline, I got an unmarked envelope with five twenty-dollar bills in it. It was exactly the $1,000 I needed. I grew, along with my team members, as I put my own needs on the line before God.

Example #4—Sacrifice

The needs that we will face as our world awareness grows cannot be responded to lightly or with a shrug of the shoulders. There will be no accurate response without cost to ourselves of both time and money.

It is difficult to talk to youth leaders about sacrifice because many are subsisting on the salaries or stipends they receive already. But maybe this is the sacrifice we start with. Without trying to sound self-pitying, perhaps we need to explain to students that ministry itself involves sacrifice.

A few years ago, I went to my high school reunion. I came home a little dejected because others were talking of their well-paying jobs, their new homes, and their promotions to upper-level management. When they asked me what I was doing, the answer "Youth worker" usually got a few snickers.

I used this occasion to teach the high schoolers I was working with that ministry and obedience involves cost and sacrifice. I explained to them that I never regretted my decisions to follow the Lord, but experiences like the high school reunion reminded me that some things must be sacrificed—like desires for power or wealth or prestige—when we follow the Lord.

Example #5—World Concern

The pastor's office should have a map and a bulletin board with missionary prayer letters on it, but what about the youth pastor's? Shouldn't we be exemplifying world concern if we in turn are supposed to be pacesetters in the youth ministry?

Consider a few practical ways to express world concern in our lives:

• supporting an orphan through World Vision or some other child-care organization,
• corresponding with missionaries,
• filling our office walls with maps, pictures of the youth group in service, or trinkets from other cultures,
• praying with regularity for someone in another part of the world,
• starting each meeting with the prayer, "Lord, thank You for the freedom that we have to meet safely in this country," as an expression of spiritual solidarity with Christians in oppressed lands,
• befriending an international student,
• reading a missionary biography and using it as an example in a lesson,
• leading on youth service projects,
• setting service projects as a priority for your family,
• learning about some new part of the world.

Many youth workers will look at such a list with a "Yes, but" hesitation. The schedule is already so busy that there is no time to add one more thing. To this, I offer two responses right out of my own life. First, start by implementing just one idea. If world missions is going to be a concern that we exemplify, we must make priority choices, and most of us have space to add at least one of these ideas.

Second, make missions your hobby. Over the course of my youth work here at Grace Chapel, I have made missions—including correspondence, geographical knowledge, and even missions news—my hobby. Together, my wife and I have devoted ourselves to trying to integrate our missions commitment into daily living in such a way that we are always learning about it.

When Paul the apostle wrote to the Philippians, he closed his letter with a reference to his personal example before them: "Whatever you have *learned* or *received* or *heard* from me, or *seen* in me—put it into practice" (Philippians 4:9). Paul was an ultimate example to the people of Philippi, and as such, he challenged others to learn from him.

We may never feel as thorough of an example as Paul seemed to be, but we can still offer ourselves as "living sacrifices" (Romans 12:1) to God and trust that He will use our lives to influence the young people under our care.

NOTES

[1]Bob Pierce, *Emphasizing Missions in the Local Church* (Grand Rapids, Michigan: Zondervan, 1964), p. 81.

[2]Taken from Tony Campolo, *Ideas for Social Action* (Grand Rapids, Michigan: Zondervan/Youth Specialties, 1984), p. 24.

[3]*Youthworker Journal* (Spring 1986), p. 67.

[4]Interview with Rick Johnson entitled "Risking All for God," *Youthworker Journal* (Spring 1986), p. 69.

CHAPTER FIVE
THE EXAMPLE OF PARENTS

Jeff is very interested in missionary service. As a matter of fact, he has thought of an international career of some sort for quite a few years. Now he is graduating from college, and service in missions is his first choice.

I could point to many influences on Jeff—missions-minded youth leaders, a missions-oriented church, and successful attempts at cross-cultural ministry—but these have been mere supplements to the most powerful example: his parents.

We in youth ministry enjoy discussing the potency of our effect on young people, but some day we must come to the realization that parents are still the most powerful influencers of the values, attitudes, and perspectives of the teenagers we work with.

Influencing the world view of students must also start in the home. If the parents are not willing to expand their own horizons, motivating students to grow as "world Christians" will be like swimming upstream. It can be done, but only with great strain and effort.

Kari Torjesen Malcolm speaks to the need for missions-oriented homes in her book *Building Your Family to Last*:

> Because world consciousness was first lost in the family, that is where it has to be regained. Christian offspring are produced in the family, and that's the most natural place for the sharing of our faith with others. That's where the hurting people of the world will come first for healing, before they go to the church. The Christian family is also the arena where new missionaries are made, and where Christianity will be kept alive during wars and chaos and persecution.[1]

The impact of family example is felt throughout the Christian world to this day. Philip and Katherine Howard (he, the former editor of the *Sunday School Times*) had six children whom they influenced toward Christian service and missions. Philip, Jr., became a missionary to the Slavey Indians of the Northwest Territories in Canada; David became a missionary to Colombia, South America, and later directed two of the Urbana Conferences (he is now the executive director of World Evangelical Fellowship); Elisabeth (Elliot) was a missionary to the Auca Indians of Ecuador (who killed her first husband, Jim) and now is a renowned missionary speaker and writer; Virginia (DeVries) served as a missionary in the Philippines; Jim and Tom pursued other Christian ministries—the pastorate and teaching respectively.

Even the Student Volunteer Movement of the late 1800s (which will be used illustratively in chapter 6) was strongly affected by one family—the Wilders. Royal Gould Wilder exemplified the sacrifice and dedication of missionary service, and his model strongly influenced his children, Grace and Robert, leaders of that great student movement.[2]

"But," you may respond, "I am not the parent of teenagers. I am the youth worker. What can I do in affecting families to be more of a model for missionary interest and world concern?"

What Can We Encourage Them to BE?

Through newsletters, seminars, and other communications related to the youth ministry, we can encourage missions interest in the home by encouraging the parents to be growing themselves.

First, encourage parents to be "world Christians." Informed, interested parents will exemplify a zeal for world awareness that students will catch at a young age and carry with them into their teen years.

Nancy DeMoss exhorts parents:

> You will have difficulty trying to build into your children [and your young people] what they cannot see in you. All life reproduces after its kind. Parents constantly model (often subconsciously) to their children a set of life priorities and values. If your children observe you aggressively caring for the world as God does, they will be stimulated to care similarly.
>
> On the other hand, if your time and energy are consumed in making money and all your money is spent amassing material possessions, then your children's greatest ambition may become a life of affluence and ease.[3]

I can point to a number of students in our youth ministry that I consider to be exceptionally open to cross-cultural, missionary service—Jim, David, Kristen, Katie, and Kirsten—and in each case, the interest in and commitment to missions originates with parents who are seeking to expand their own world view.

Second, encourage parents to pray for their children. Jeff—the student I referred to earlier—is, in part, a product of his mother's prayers. She has lifted him up to the Lord (like the biblical examples of Hannah [1 Samuel 1:28] and Eunice [2 Timothy 1:5]), supporting him through her prayers but giving him back to the Lord.

Wendy's parents, on the other hand, exhibit a desire to withhold their daughter from the Lord. They keep her away from service projects and restrict her from the youth activities that would expose her to the "ugly" parts of our city (Boston) and our world. One wonders if they are openhanded before the Lord with their desire for their daughter.

Third, encourage parents to support their teenager's efforts. Bob and Cynthia have followed in the path of many other parents at Grace Chapel. They do not plan family vacations and other family get-togethers until the first commitments are made—mission trips and service projects. They support their children's efforts by re-arranging their own schedules as a statement of their endorsement. And their children are showing the signs of greater commitment to service than many of their peers.

John and Lilly heard of their teenager's desire to help street people on Thanksgiving Day. Rather than responding with a harsh, "Sorry . . . Thanksgiving is a *family* day," they responded by insti-tuting a new family tradition—they all went together to serve Thanksgiving dinner to street people at a soup kitchen in Boston. It was their most rewarding Thanksgiving together ever!

Ronald Kotesky states that "our society has created adolescents but has made little provision for them. It has not given them a real role to play."[4] As a result, students feel worthless and left out, and this leads to frustration. If parents can work to give their children the encouragement and example that they need to be participants, whole families will grow together.

Fourth, encourage parents to be open to missions themselves. Like youth workers, the parent who encourages his or her children to think about missionary service will face the question: "Why aren't you out there?" Every parent will face his or her own answer, but the best answer by far is, "Well, I am praying about it too."

This is why Tom and Shirley's teenagers know that missions is serious business in their home. Their parents are preparing to make a mid-career shift to go out as missionaries. The students have participated in the decision, and now—in a sort of "role reversal"—they are learning to let go of their parents to the Lord's service.

Finally, encourage parents to be witnesses. Brad is thinking of full-time Christian ministry, but he is open to any career, as long as he has the opportunity to reach out to people. He genuinely loves to share the love of Christ with others, and I know where he learned it—from his parents. His home was a place where the lonely were welcomed, the hurting comforted, and the inquiring answered. And primarily, his parents communicated that winning people to Jesus Christ was the greatest privilege on earth.

I do not know if the gifts of the Spirit are inherited in families, but, if they are, I know that Brad will have the gift of evangelism . . . because he caught it from his mom and dad.

> The homes that reach out to the wounded are often the ones that produce the best future missionaries. I believe when a child grows up sensitized not only to the needs of family members but to what's going on elsewhere, that child has a head start no educational institution can give.[5]

What Can We Encourage Them to DO?

Whenever parents catch the vision for a "world-Christian" home, they begin to ask, "Well, what can I *do* to create a greater world awareness—an international flavor—in my home?" Here are some suggestions to offer parents.

1. International decorations. Maps, world globes, and artifacts from missionaries or missionary travels all help to create a home environment that hints at the great world we are called to serve.

Larry and Linda have a world-Christian home. There are maps—on the coffee mugs, on trays, even a world-globe pillow. There are artifacts everywhere that they have collected from their missionary friends with the Wycliffe Bible Translators, as well as from their own travels overseas. World geography games, international pictures, and a variety of other visual stimuli affect anyone who visits their home. These decorations are part of the reason that their children have grown up thinking about international ministry.

2. Missionary correspondence. I cannot remember much about my parent's correspondence with missionaries during my childhood, but I do remember the stamps. When a missionary letter came, it meant an exotic picture, a bright blue butterfly or an African animal on the stamp. The visual impact of the stamp gave me a positive excitement about missions.

Parents who correspond with missionaries set an example to their teenagers in several ways. They demonstrate their support of those overseas by encouragement. They take the time to write, and this communicates that the parents are willing to do their part in the world task. The correspondence also serves as a catalyst for family prayer, which in turn involves the children.

3. Host missionaries or international visitors. International students, high school exchange students, or visiting missionaries can all bring a taste of the world to any home. Parents who desire to teach their students to reach out across cultures and to learn from others of a different country can do so by inviting these people into their home. "One of the great gifts we can give our children from the start is friendship with people from all different races, countries, and walks of life."[6]

4. Adopt a child. Many organizations offer opportunities to support children from all over the world. Some of these children are orphans, while others are simply from impoverished families who cannot offer sufficient support. For about $20 per month, a family can adopt a supported child, leading to an international learning experience for all family members.

One family's adopted child provides them an opportunity to discover more about the needs in Kenya and East Africa. Another has tried to teach family members a few basic written phrases of greeting so that they can write to their child in his native language.

Perhaps the most potent example is the Collins family. They were living on a rather tight budget, but—like many families in their neighborhoods—they managed to squeeze out enough money each month to subscribe to cable TV. When they learned of the need to support children overseas, they realized that they could not respond without cutting back somewhere else. As a family, they decided to cancel their cable TV subscription so that they could support an orphaned child. A simple sacrifice, perhaps, but it communicated to the family members that being a world Christian means giving up some of the things that our society says we "need."

Two additional truths should be communicated to parents to maximize the impact of the example in the home. *First*, we should encourage parents to *start young*. The children that grow up on an "diet" of international exposure, example, and experience have a much greater ability to grow into being world Christians.

Robyne and David Bryant discuss their efforts in rearing their world Christians this way:

> Building a world-Christian vision into family life is basically the same as integrating a world-Christian philosophy throughout one's own life. But with children in the picture we are pressed to be certain the journey is far more tangible than merely philosophical. A sensory approach works for us.[7]

For the Bryants, building a world-Christian lifestyle at home involves the five senses at work:
- sight—picture books that show people from all over the world,
- hearing—tapes of music from other lands as well as exposure to foreign languages,
- smell and taste—foreign foods (especially desserts to get young children motivated!),
- touch—playing with artifacts from other lands or actually touching people in need through missions service.[8]

A *second* truth that needs to be communicated relates to *the long-term impact*. A world-Christian home environment does not guarantee that all of the children will become missionaries (any more than a Christian home environment guarantees that all of the children will become Christians). Nevertheless, a home that emphasizes world concern is more likely to produce young people who are sensitive to their role in meeting world needs. Kari Torjesen Malcolm again provides us with the needed encouragement:

> The only place where the attitude toward people from other races is going to change is in the home. Thank God for homes that have taken in foreign students as members of the family, written regularly to them when they return to their homelands, and later visited them. Children from such homes are rich spiritually compared to those who have never had a foreigner eat at their table.
>
> The Mitchells are such a family that trained their children with world awareness from the start. The result was that five out of the six children went to the mission field—to Indonesia, India, Japan, Hong Kong, Ethiopia, Kenya, and Trinidad. The sixth one helped his parents with the mission board they founded. The father used to say, "The only thing we can bring to heaven with us is our children."[9]

NOTES

[1]Kari Torjesen Malcolm, *Building Your Family to Last* (Downers Grove, Illinois: InterVarsity Press, 1987), p. 119.

[2]Timothy C. Wallstrom, *The Creation of a Student Movement to Evangelize the World* (Pasadena, California: William Carey Library, 1980), pp. 77–78.

[3]Nancy DeMoss, "How to Give Your Children a Heart for the World," *Worldwide Challenge* (September 1978), p. 19.

[4]Ronald Kotesky, *Understanding Adolescence* (Wheaton, Illinois: Victor Books, 1987), p. 31.

[5]Malcolm, *Building your Family*, p. 127.

[6]Malcolm, *Building your Family*, p. 125.

[7]Robyne Bryant, "Teach the Vision," *World Christian* (July/August 1987), p. 36.

[8]*Ibid.*

[9]Malcolm, *Building your Family*, p. 128.

CHAPTER SIX
THE EXAMPLE OF PEERS

The desire for a small circle of friends is a powerful force at work in the lives of today's teenager. The group—in which students find security and love—is one of the prime motivators in the lives of young people.

So why not use this reality for good?

Peer influence is often frowned upon by youth leaders as a totally negative opponent to the advance of the Gospel in the lives of students, or to discipleship or missions. I would rather have us look at peer influence as a neutral factor which can affect students either positively or negatively, depending on the shift.

The Student Volunteer Movement of the late 1800s and early 1900s produced thousands of missionaries and many mission leaders who stayed here in the United States and Canada to influence others. The Student Volunteer Movement was a peer movement. Although the initial vision was affected by the great missioner Royal Gould Wilder, it was primarily a student movement of young people motivating each other:

> Personal example was a most important aspect of the missionary appeal. The student volunteer was a colleague, a peer, an equal in age and ability, who had already taken the foolish step he was advocating. He could therefore encourage his companions to "come," a much more persuasive request than "go."[1]

In simple terms, I call this positive peer pressure. When the "group" is headed in a productive direction and the force of the "group" encourages others to join in, the pressure exerted on the individual is positive. Those who join in as a result of the group's pressure must, at some time, come to make a personal commitment to the vision, but the initial involvement may simply be a result of a student's desire to be accepted.

Over the ten years of missions emphasis in our youth ministry, we have experienced this positive peer pressure at work. Over the years, student involvement overseas has become so commonplace that students without international experience have sought it (and we have tried to make it financially possible for them to get it). This has been a positive directive which has stirred great mission activity. (At one point, over 60 percent of our youth group members had served overseas or cross-culturally in this country.)

Positive peer pressure has also had its drawbacks. If the *only* reason to go and serve is to gain peer acceptance (i.e., the personal commitment to the vision is never made—then the service ideal can degenerate into another social activity.

Encouraging Peer Influence

Almost every youth group will have at least a few students who are motivated to expand their world views. Family background, personal experience, or even reading about the adventures of others can stir students' desire to know more about the world.

These students, however, may never make their interests or desires known without our encouragement. In addition, the potential of their influencing their peers is lost if we fail to offer them the boost they need.

Here are a few ideas to build up the missions-minded students and help them touch their peers.

1. *Affirmation.* When Mark went around the world with his dad, we took time out of the youth Sunday School to interview him about his experiences in China, Korea, East Germany, and England. We made him a minihero in the eyes of youth group members.

Earl gave an interview to his school paper about his experiences as a "missionary" in Ecuador. When the article was published, we highlighted it in the youth group. We wanted his positive example to be made known to others.

Referring to Pastor Von Trutschler again, Rick Johnson summarized the impact of affirmation on him as a high school student. When he and his friend expressed their desire to serve as missionaries, "everyone except Pastor Von told us that we were crazy, we were too young, we should wait and go through Bible school, we should go to seminary—and *then* think about the mission field."[2]

2. *Moderation.* When a student voices a desire to pursue God's call—even to the point of missionary service—we can overreact in our desire to affirm. We may push too hard and give the student

more than he or she can handle. The potential for leadership and affecting others may be there, but we must be careful not to launch the willing student into notoriety so fast that he is overcome by pride (see 1 Timothy 3:6) or she is put in the position of making commitments which she cannot fulfill.

Several of our youth leaders were looking for students who were open to the idea of reaching across cultures into the urban areas of Boston. When the students responded favorably, the leaders responded wisely. Rather than overdoing the students' willingness by committing them to ministries in which the students would feel overwhelmed, the leaders organized a small basketball team which enrolled in an urban league.

The leaders even went a step further in moderation: they made clear to the players that the goal was to build some relationships with high school students from the city, not win. The decision was a wise one. The team lost every game, but they accomplished their goal.

Encouraging missions interest in students does not mean overloading them with too many responsibilities too soon. It means matching missions involvement with their missions motivation; this is moderation.

3. *Teamwork.* Perhaps the best way to encourage peer influence toward greater world awareness is to get the students working in teams. In a team effort, the least motivated and the most motivated might get paired together, and the example of the stronger student can rub off.

Two of our high school students were very motivated to be involved in the care of international children at a conference that our church was hosting. We probably could have gotten by with just these two as the child-care personnel, but we decided to encourage them to stimulate others to be involved. They brought along four friends and, working together, they cared for almost two dozen children from eleven countries—learning about those countries in the process. The teamwork served as a motivator for the students who were less interested in international matters.

4. *Special treatment.* Over the course of my leadership with young people, I have tried to give special treatment to the students who have had unique experiences related to other cultures. If a student is bilingual, he might be singled out as the most brilliant guy at the meeting. International students are given a special welcome and are then invited to quiz us about their country. Students who have grown up overseas (missionary children, military children,

or the children of executives who work overseas) are invited to share the most exciting experiences of their overseas experiences—from climbing Mount Kilimanjaro to living through a typhoon, from shopping in Paris to eating snails.

Our intent is twofold. We want to make the student of exceptional experience feel welcome and not "foreign." (We want them to know that we are interested in their lives.) Also, we want to stir a positive desire to learn and discover in students who are the "youth group regulars."

The positive example of peers occurs best in a youth ministry where there is a positive thrust toward discipleship. In this context, students are being taught that we should be Christlike models toward each other, and they can then respond by their growth toward a greater world awareness.

NOTES
[1]Timothy C. Wallstrom, *The Creation of a Student Movement to Evangelize the World* (Pasadena, California: William Carey Library, 1980), pp. 13–14.

[2]Rick Johnson interview, "Risking All for God," *Youthworker Journal* (Spring 1986), p. 68.

CHAPTER SEVEN
THE EXAMPLE OF MISSIONARIES

The final group that can provide excellent examples and role models to youth group members are missionaries who visit our churches and our youth ministries. When positively plugged into a program, missionaries provide students with a picture of what it means to be committed through a career to the task of the Great Commission.

There is also a remedial reason to incorporate missionaries in the youth ministry. Many of our Christian young people have formed negative stereotypes about missionaries which we can work to dispel through positive examples. Virginia Anderson sums up the two most prevalent stereotypes this way:

> What is your idea of a missionary? Maybe you think of a missionary as a dull, outdated dud who goes to the mission field because he cannot succeed in his own country. Or perhaps you think missionaries are all dedicated, heroic beings who have gone the last mile in self-sacrifice and are just a few steps short of sinless perfection.[1]

Although there may be some missionaries that we encounter who will substantiate such images on either extreme, the average missionary will be just that—average. If we can show our young people that missionaries are people just like us, who have been summoned by God for service in some other part of our world (or in some special task), then we will have maximized the impact of the missionary example.

Some Ways Not to Use Missionaries

Providing models of obedience to the young people through the presentation of missionaries must be tempered by a realistic estimate of both our youth and our missionaries. Over the course of the involvement of many cross-cultural workers in our youth ministry, we have made some errors that can be avoided.

• *Don't* use a missionary as a speaker if he or she is not a good communicator. In the past, we assumed that every missionary had the gift of oral communication; we no longer make this mistake. Some are more nervous in front of a group of high schoolers than a junior higher would be in front of our worship service. Others drone on with no sensitivity at all to the audience. The net results? Students think that missionaries are, at best, boring and, at worst, out of touch with the world around them.

We had Steve as a speaker at our youth group, and he actually did quite well; he is a good communicator. But he was over the heads of our young people. We would have been wise to have asked him before he came to the church if he was comfortable speaking to youth. I learned later that he was terrified of teenagers and preferred speaking to older adults. Being with young people was, in his words, "out of my league."

• *Don't* include missionaries as members of the youth leadership team if they do not like teenagers. When missionaries are on furlough, they are sometimes looking for opportunities to serve in the church. One of the areas in need is often the youth staff team, and the missionaries are sent our way.

This assignment is, for some, a greater cultural assignment than they can adjust to. The language, priorities, music, and lifestyle of teenagers may be so foreign to the missionaries that they get frustrated or even angry at the youth. The better solution is to guide missionaries into areas of service where they feel equipped.

• *Don't* use missionaries without briefing them first. One woman came home on furlough and met with our youth group. She was a good communicator and fairly effective with teenagers, but she gave our group the same talk that she would have given at prayer meeting: too many slides, too long, and too technical.

She needed an edited version, with more stories that might have interested teenagers, and with more time for personal interaction (see below). Her presentation was poorly received because we failed to brief her beforehand on how to be more effective in speaking to our youth. (Incidentally, missionaries have often commented that they welcome any briefing that we can offer. They desire to be effective, and we know the students best; so we can tell them how to increase their effectiveness.)

• *Don't* assume that missionaries will make good coworkers. It is sad to say that some of the worst missionary examples that our youth have seen have come from missionaries who practiced a "Do as I say, not as I do" style of leadership. In mission service projects, we have often encouraged missionaries to work alongside of us. In *most* cases, the missionaries have been pacesetting workers, exemplifying a positive spirit in the work, and providing great models of servanthood.

But in the examples of Bill, Dan, and John, their "co-work" was actually counterproductive. In spite of the fact that these missionaries had helped organize our projects, their unwillingness to tackle them with us had a negative impact on the students. In the case of Bill, he stood around giving orders, but he was never willing to pick up a paintbrush. In the case of Dan, he always managed to disappear during work hours and reappear at snack-time and on the days off. John worked with us, but he spent more time worrying about his tools and our use of them than he did working. All were unfortunate examples that left students with negative images of the missionaries as workers.

In each case, we tried to communicate with the missionaries what they were exemplifying, but it probably would have been better for our students if the missionaries had just stayed away from the work site.

Effective Use of Missionaries in the Group

The negative examples above should not paint a picture that causes youth workers to be wary of missionaries; instead, it should help us be realistic and honest about ways to maximize their impact.

For this purpose, consider several "DO'S" related to the example of missionaries:

• *Do* use missionaries as youth group participants. When Steve (referred to earlier) came to the youth group, his talk went over the heads of the students, but he still managed to impress them. He stayed on after the talk, joked with students over refreshments, and performed well as a member of an informal volleyball team. His participation was the primary example he offered, and one student commented later, "You know, he was pretty normal for a missionary."

Both Steve and I agreed that to be "pretty normal" was a compliment.

• *Do* use missionaries as educators about missionary life. Sometimes our missions presentations leave people with the impression that missionary life is one exciting event after another. For most missionaries, this is not the case.

Kevin and Roberta were the educators that were honest enough with our students to communicate what life in another culture is *really* like. They told of the frustration of being incapable of communication, the loneliness of family separation over the holidays, and the fears that they had for their children. They told the truth about day-to-day missionary life—sometimes it is pretty "average" and you just go about your routines believing that God has called you there for a purpose.

One student wrote about the impact of Kevin and Roberta: "From them I learned that missionaries are average people who obey God by going to another culture. In that culture, they still have a family, a dog, and a place to live, and they try to adjust so that they can tell others about the love of Christ."

• *Do* use missionaries as motivators toward a life of faith. Chuck came to our youth group as a veteran missionary with over 20 years of experience. I was fearful that his age could make him ineffective with the teenagers, but I was wrong. He held the students spellbound as he told them of the adventure of faith—trusting God as a way of life.

At one point, he told the students of his escape during the Congolese rebellion in Zaire when his partner in ministry, Dr. Paul Carlson, was shot in the back as Chuck pulled him over a wall. At another point, he had the students rolling with laughter as he described an encounter in northeastern Zaire with several mountain gorillas. Standing face-to-face, Chuck versus the gorillas, he stared them down as they beat their chests in protest to his presence.

From a very serious moment to a humorous one, Chuck's message to the students was clear—missionary living is taking God at His word and trusting Him, even when the circumstances are seemingly against you.

A Life-changing Example

When using missionaries as examples, it is helpful to use the guidelines listed above, but do not be bound by them. Some exceptional things can happen, even when these ideals are not met. Many of our missionary partners will come with words empowered by the Holy Spirit.

Bruce Olson, whose story of faith is recorded in his book, *Bruchko*, shares one such story about the life-changing power of the example of a missionary in his life. He describes one of the missionaries, Mr. Rayburn, who "served" in New Guinea. He was a short, dumpy man wearing a bright green polka-dot shirt, black pants, and dirty tennis shoes. Bruce was surprised that anyone would dress that sloppily to speak in church, but he soon discovered that Mr. Rayburn had a forceful message.

> . . . Mr. Rayburn showed movies that he had taken. In one scene, a man was eating a rat. You could just see the tail of the rat hanging out of the man's mouth—then, phht, it was gone.
>
> There were other pictures: some of extreme poverty in the midst of modern cities, some of "natives" and their odd clothes, houses, and eating habits. Then Mr. Rayburn made his appeal.
>
> "These people are starving, dying of disease, living in ignorance, eating rats. But most of all they are starving for the knowledge of Jesus Christ. They are dying *lost*, without knowing how Jesus Christ can save them from their sins. Can you sit comfortably in your seats and accept that? Do you care about these men and women, living in squalor and filth? They're dying, damned to eternal condemnation! And what do you do? Maybe if you're really virtuous you put a little money in the collection plate on Sunday morning. Maybe you put in a dollar to reach these people starving for the Gospel.
>
> "But Jesus wants more of you. He wants more than your lip service to the great cause of missions. It's your responsibility to take the Gospel of Christ to these people."[2]

On that night—in spite of the external factors which might not have been perfect—God spoke to Bruce Olson, and he ended up taking the Gospel to a South American tribe much like the one reached by Mr. Rayburn.

We are wise never to underestimate the impact of a missionary example on our students' lives (and on our own).

NOTES

[1]Virginia Anderson, *Making Missions Meaningful* (Wheaton, Illinois: Pioneer Girls, 1966), p. 14.

[2]Bruce Olson, *Bruchko* (Carol Stream, Illinois: Creation House, 1978), pp. 35–36.

Section
Three

EXPANDING YOUR STUDENTS' WORLD VIEW
Basic Ingredient #2—Exposure

Our friend April works in a greenhouse. My wife and I do not understand too much about flowers and the way that they grow, but we have learned from watching April and her coworkers that "creating a growing environment" is critically important to their business.

In the flower business, the environment involves heat, light, fertilizers, pesticides, and water. In the business of youth ministry, there is another distinctive environment. Working with teenagers—creating an environment where they can grow—involves relevant teaching, experiences in Christian obedience, and effective modeling. In this climate, students can thrive like flowers in a greenhouse.

The specific environment for missions is a particular challenge in youth ministry because we are taking students from the world in which they live into a world beyond their sphere of experience.

The starting point, however, is with us, the youth leaders—not the students. If we are to create a "mood for missions" in our youth ministries, we must be leading the way through our examples. The adage "More things are *caught* than are taught" certainly applies to this matter of an expanded world view.

Secondly, a missions "mood" is not created in a once-a-year activity or through a summer mission team. The best missions awareness in a youth ministry occurs when a group (and the leaders) are consistently thinking about evangelism, discipleship, and the fulfillment of the Great Commission (Matthew 28:18-20). A one-time spurt of missions involvement may make us feel like "world Christian" youth leaders, but a year-round missions education will produce the best long-term results.

CHAPTER EIGHT
EXPOSURE IN THE CHURCH

Dr. Terry Hulbert of the Columbia Bible College and Seminary has a ministry of encouraging churches to grow in their world view and in their role in the fulfillment of the Great Commission. In an address to the Association of Church Missions Committees' National Conference in 1984, he challenged churches to work toward the creation of the missionary-growing environment.

> One of the greatest contributions the local church can make to worldwide evangelization is not just by giving money, but by growing missionaries. By modeling, teaching, training, motivating, counseling, encouraging, informing, and challenging people from their early years into the teens and right through college, the church can move them right up to the launching pad from which they are propelled into the orbit of a cross-cultural ministry.[1]

Many churches are developing a vision for home-grown missionaries that will be stimulating not only to the missionary force but also to the churches involved.

Growing our own missionaries is one of the top three goals of our missions committee, and the goal has been reaffirmed as we have seen people go out from our church. Marc gained a vision for missions through our church, was partially trained at our church, and was then sent off by our church. The benefits of this cooperative process have been experienced by our entire church, not by just Marc.

This sending process, however, is a churchwide effort, and to accomplish it, we must be working in the entire fellowship to keep people exposed to the opportunities, needs, and challenges of cross-cultural ministry.

To have the maximum impact on young people and adults, church leaders must not limit themselves to some conference, missions seminar, or vision-building film. The creation of a mission "mood" is more than that. It is the regular affirmation—by word and deed—of the foundational statements underlying missions which will provide the best long-term exposure to attenders, both young and old.

Reaching Nonbelievers Is a Priority

For the church that fills its schedule with social activities and events that entertain the "saints," the challenge is evident. If we have activities, programs, sermons, and educational opportunities which are *all* directed at the Christian community, the implicit message is clear: the church may be as selfish as the "world" out of which the members have come.

Frank Tillapaugh is credited with making the analogy of the local church as an aquarium. His observation is that many churches are spending their time keeping the "fish" safe and protected in the aquarium rather than making its members reach out as "fishers of men." Will our churches be keepers of the aquarium or "fishers" for lost humanity?

If indeed our churches degenerate to the point of self-preoccupation (even if this preoccupation is related to "good" things, like Christian growth), the missions vision is lost. Communicating to members that "reaching the lost" overseas is a priority will fall on deaf ears if reaching the lost in our own neighborhoods is not being taught or exemplified.

On the other hand, the church with evangelistic training, neighborhood Bible studies, and a strong outward thrust will have an easier time communicating a vision for worldwide outreach. If Christians learn that they are being built up in the church *so that* they can reach out in the "work of the ministry" (see Ephesians 4:11-13), the environment for evangelism will be cultivated.

Sending People Is a Priority

Through public affirmation of missionaries, a significant missions budget, and a high profile of the missions family, the church communicates to its members its commitment that those who are sent will be supported.

In Acts 13 we see how the church illustrated this priority by the sending of Saul (later Paul) and Barnabas. When the Holy Spirit directed them to release Saul and Barnabas, the church obeyed— even though it meant that they would lose 40 percent of their leadership. The church incurred the cost of personnel loss because they believed in the sending vision.

Over the past few years, we have "lost" youth workers, evangelism trainers, and Bible study leaders in the sending process, but the open-handed enthusiasm of our church leadership has communicated a desire to release people to ministries beyond ourselves. The outward orientation has been affirmed by commissioning people to leave.

One of the best sending stories comes from the Austin family. Charlie and Linda (the parents) encouraged their children to go out in service. As a result, both Lisa and Amy went out as teenagers on summer projects—Lisa to a Navajo reservation, Amy to a ministry in Haiti. Amy communicated her experience to her grandmother, Marion, a leader in our women's Bible study ministry. Marion, in turn, decided to use her 30-plus years of food service experience in missions, and, as a result, has been using her retirement years to assist in a children's feeding program in Haiti at which she has coordinated the feeding of as many as 2,000 children per week. Charlie and Linda sent their children; the Austin family sent their grandmother; and the church sent them all.

Worship Is a Priority

Venturing out into missions without a strong base of worship and prayer is like trying to build a skyscraper without the architect and the plans. We will get frustrated because we will not be sure of who is in charge, and we will not know where to start or how to build.

The best missions-oriented churches are those that communicate a strong sense of worship. The attention of members is first of all pointed to the *Lord* of the harvest (Matthew 9:36-39) because *He* is the only source of power, wisdom, and direction for the great task before them.

The ending point of missions will be worship. At the throne of God, John the Apostle saw "a great multitude that no one could count, from every nation, tribe, people, and language" (Revelation 7:9).

The starting point, therefore, should likewise be worship. Isaiah's call starts with worship: "Holy, holy, holy is the Lord Almighty; the whole earth is full of His glory" (Isaiah 6:3). The magnificence of God leads to humility and repentance: " 'Woe to me!' I cried, 'I am ruined! For I am a man of unclean lips . . . and my eyes have seen the King, the Lord Almighty" (Isaiah 6:5). *Only after this,* God calls

Isaiah out, and he responds obediently, "Here am I. Send me" (Isaiah 6:8).

If this worship of the Almighty is communicated through our church experiences, members will be able to understand that our call to missions is not in response to a weak God who desperately needs our help. Instead, we will see the majesty of God and respond to Him as the Lord, the Boss, the Commander of the kingdom forces.

Missions Education Is a Priority

Any church leader, youth pastor, or Sunday School educator knows that there are many educational curricula to choose from. Each has its varied strengths and weaknesses, and leaders must make the choices based on the best resources for their particular educational situation.

For a good missions environment, however, educational materials must be chosen based on which provide (or, more realistically, allow for the supplementation of) missions education materials. When all of the people in Sunday School are being educated regarding the Great Commission and God's call into all the world, growing together as world Christians becomes a unified effort.

In our efforts to provide educational foundations for missions involvement, our church and many others are pursuing a variety of options, such as:

• each Sunday School class having an "adopted" missionary,

• each Sunday School class integrating missions learning into the existing curriculum,

• class projects to raise money for (or otherwise support) mission projects or missionaries,

• allowing missions speakers into the Sunday School schedule,

• providing maps, flags, or other visual reminders in the classrooms,

• arranging class coordinators who can correspond with missionaries, send birthday, Christmas, or other greeting cards, and bring prayer needs before the whole class.

We are fortunate in that our church educators have made missions-learning a priority every year. As a result, children from two-years-old upward are taught regularly about missionaries, other countries, and the varied picture of God's church around the world. As these students grow, they will be knowledgeable about and open to the call to be world Christians.

How Churches Can Provide Missions Exposure to Youth

The four foundational statements will help teenagers realize that missions is a priority for the entire church, but there are other actions that pastors and church leaders can take to let students know that they have a part in the world of missions. What follows are a few ideas which we have tried or have learned from others.

1. *Have the youth pastor speak on missions in the worship service.* This communicates to the young people that (a) the church believes in the youth ministry; (b) the youth group and the vision for missions go together; and (c) the youth pastor is seen as an integral part of the sending process.

2. *Involve students in missions services.* Some may offer reports of short-term experiences, while others may simply share how the youth group is praying for missions. We have had students carry flags in a flag processional at the missions conference, participate in a drama-team skit related to missions, and provide the special music with a missions hymn. When students are allowed and encouraged to participate, they will feel that missions is a churchwide effort, not just an adult activity which they watch.

3. *Orient some programs to youth culture.* Missions exposure in the church at large does not mean segregating the students in their own meetings all the time. There must be time for the students to see that they are important enough to the church to warrant special attention. This may mean a night at the missions conference when there is contemporary music, activity-oriented learning, and even decorations which students would like.

Doing this will require flexibility on behalf of the adults, but it will be a strong message of love and acceptance to the young people. It will say to them, in effect, "We want you to see how important you are in the missions vision of this church."

4. *Involve students in the missions leadership.* When I visit churches who ask me, "How can we reach our young people?" I am frequently amazed at the fact that they have never talked about this with the young people of the church. If we do not want our missions conference to be boring to teenagers, why not invite two or three to serve on the planning committee? If we hope to direct our missions efforts toward recruiting youth, why not include a couple of young people on the missions committee? Some students will not speak up, and others may make some outrageous suggestions, but the problems associated with involving students should not prevent our efforts. If we want to reach teenagers, why not involve them more

and get their ideas?

Creating a missions environment in the local church will take much effort and often years of work, but it can be done. When the church leadership, Sunday School educators, and youth leaders are all working together to lead people toward an outward orientation, the openness to world missions will grow.

Creating this missions environment is an active choice that pastors and church leaders must make, especially if teenagers are going to be touched. Tony Campolo discussed the choice facing pastors in his book *Ideas for Social Action:*

> Recently I discussed with a local pastor the ministry which his church has had with young people. He was frustrated and discouraged because his church did not seem to be able to hold on to its youth in spite of a host of efforts. His church supported parties, concerts, camping trips, and a variety of other activities aimed at enticing young people and getting their support. Nothing his church did achieved the desired results. In exasperation, he threw up his hands and asked, "What do we have to do for young people in order to attract them?"
>
> "Perhaps," I said, "young people are not attracted so much by a church that tries to entertain them as they are attracted to a church that challenges them to do things for others. If your church provided concrete ways for young people to minister to the needs of others and to effect social change in the world, they would find your church very attractive. Young people just may be looking for a church that appeals to their latent idealism by calling them to be agents of God's revolution and to be part of His movement to bring healing and justice to His broken world." I believe that the church that calls young people to engage in ministry to the community by helping the poor, working for racial equality, caring for the elderly, and improving life for the disadvantaged will find that it will attract numerous young people who are looking for the fulfillment that comes from investing their lives in the service of others.[2]

If we make this choice in our churches, the vision of homegrown missionaries, as well as a church filled with world Christians, will become a reality.

NOTES

[1]Terry Hulbert, *Discipling Leaders with a Vision for the World* (Coral Gables, Florida: Worldteam, 1984), p. 7.

[2]Tony Campolo, *Ideas for Social Action* (Grand Rapids, Michigan: Zondervan/Youth Specialties, 1983), pp. 9–10.

CHAPTER NINE
EXPOSURE IN THE YOUTH GROUP

The goal of expanding the world view of the students in our youth ministries will only be achieved through consistent, sustained exposure to the world beyond ourselves. The best way for the youth group to be exposed to missionary service is for youth leaders to be exposed to missionary service. "Whatever is most on your heart will be most on your lips." If youth leaders seriously pray about world missions, think about missions, study about the world, read news magazines, or pursue other types of missions input, then these leaders will have a worldwide perspective that can be transferred to the group.

Before proceeding into some specific ideas to foster this exposure, let's define the idea. For our purposes, "exposure in the youth group" should be defined as follows:

> Providing educational and learning opportunities in the youth ministry program which will open students' eyes to world needs, familiarize them with the world of missions, and give them opportunities to respond.

With this definition in mind, then, consider a number of ways to expose the youth group to the world.

Quizzes, games, crosswords, and more. The most basic starting point of familiarity with missions and world issues may be in the Sunday School class or the weekly Bible study. In this context, students expect more of a "classroom" format, so they will be more accepting of learning devices like quizzes. (See sample quiz at the end of this chapter.)

In our youth ministry, global quizzes became something of a tradition. There were usually questions about world events, people in missions history, geographical questions, and even some more personal questions related to the church's missionary family.

The intent of a quiz is not to overwhelm students with their lack of knowledge, but rather to stir them to learn. For this reason, "grading" or sharing answers publicly may not be wise. Instead, make the quiz a group learning experience or have the students work in teams.

Missionary or world-awareness games are now becoming available as our secular educators realize that many Americans are geographically ignorant. *Where in the World*[1]—a geographical board game—global map flash cards, and "Trivial Pursuit"-type questions can all be fun in the youth group where world awareness is encouraged.

We have even made up our own games. One example is a game that requires only a map of the world (which is held by the game referee). The referee calls out a country name. The student (or team of students) then writes the answers to three questions: (1) What continent? (2) One neighboring country? and (3) What's the capital? Each answer is worth five points, and those that are more geographically aware will win, but all can benefit.

Crossword puzzles, matching lists of people and countries, and other creative lessons on missions knowledge can help in the ongoing exposure process. Good exposure must balance knowledge and humor. The quizzes or games can be educational, but they should also be entertaining or we will lose the student's interest. Motivational leadership will make the learning tool effective.

I was recently reminded how well these devices do work. I was with a student who had graduated from our youth ministry six years earlier, and he was talking about these quizzes which we offered twice per year. He told me, "By the time we graduated the youth group, we all knew at least two things about missions. We knew that Ulan Bator was the capital of Mongolia and that Paul and Christie wanted to go to the Great Wall of China."

How did the students know this? Those two questions—"What is the capital of Mongolia?" and "What location on earth do Paul and Christie want to visit?"—appeared in some form on every quiz. By the time a student graduated, he or she had seen these questions six to eight times.

Stimulation learning. Role playing has become an accepted way to communicate truth—or, better, to allow students to discover truths for themselves. We have tried a variety of simulation learning techniques, but three examples will suffice to give an overview of the possibilities.

"Refugee Camp." This is a program coordinated by World Concern[2] designed to help students understand the frustrations of living in and surviving the hardships of a refugee camp. The simple pro-

grams, dry, starchy food, and sheer boredom of subsisting at a refugee camp were simulated for 24 hours. Together, students learned what it is like to be bored, helpless, and even hopeless in a refugee camp environment.

"Underground Church." This is an activity where the youth group meeting simulates the meeting of a church in a communist country. Meeting by candlelight, quoting (rather than reading) Scriptures, entering the meeting with a "code" word, or having the meeting interrupted by the governmental authorities can all help young people gain a greater sensitivity to Christians who meet at the risk of their careers or lives.

Our best "underground church" simulation occurred when we met in a youth facility away from the church grounds. We instructed students *not* to come to the building. Instead, they were met a block away by their "contact" who gave them a code word for entry. Then, in groups of two, they were instructed to walk discreetly to the cellar door. They were met by someone who asked the code word. Their answer got them into a cold basement room which was lit only by candles.

After the group was in place, the "service" began with songs (from memory), Scripture (from memory), and a testimony offered by someone who had really been to Eastern Europe the summer before. There was then a birthday cake (as some churches meet under the guise of birthday celebrations). We closed with conversational prayer for Christians in various Eastern block countries.[3]

"Missions Roulette." This event can happen anytime, but we have used the idea most during our missions conference. Using a globe on a spinning axis, we spin the "world" and have the small groups' leaders point to a spot. This is the location where their group will go as missionaries. (Remember to tell them that they go to the nearest landmass; if you do not tell them this, two thirds of the groups will end up in the oceans of the world.)

The groups have time to prepare to be missionaries, and then they put on a skit of what missionaries in their country will face. To make roulette effective, small group leaders should be briefed beforehand about some of the major regions of the world. We have found this simulation most effective when missions leaders are available to answer questions about various parts of the world. When this is not possible, we have given the groups books to use like *Operation World*[4] or the *World Christian Encyclopedia.*[5] These can provide basic background information.

Fund-Raisers. A variety of organizations have excellent fund-raising programs which youth groups can use in the exposure-to-missions process. World Vision's "Planned Famine" or "Love Loaf" programs,[6] the "Compassion Project" of Compassion International,[7] and a variety of other projects can help the youth group learn about and do something in response to missions.[8]

Simple cross-cultural experiences. A few summers ago, we realized that our students were very narrow-sighted in their suburban culture. Even though some had traveled overseas, a number were very unaware of the inner city of Boston, our near neighbor.

We took them to an urban mission organization, the Emmanuel Gospel Center, for a weekend of life in the city. This cross-cultural experience pushed our students in one fundamental direction: it helped to destroy their stereotypes.

The weekend started with a lecture from one of the leaders on how to develop a positive appreciation for the city. He explained our stereotypes, taught us the errors of our viewpoints, and helped us grow by sending us out to register our opinions. (See the sample handout we were given.)

Other churches may try creative methods of involvement which can stimulate cross-cultural appreciation. Exchanges of youth groups (inner-city group visits suburban group, or *vice versa*; Armenian youth group visits Chinese youth group, etc.), international meals, or even involvement in local neighborhoods that are usually untouched by our churches[9] can all build a greater world view in the youth ministry.

Writing prayers/writing letters. Whenever we begin to expose our young people to the needs of the world, they start asking, "What can I do?" Even though we want to get them involved, the best spiritual exposure we can give them is to turn them upward—to help them realize that God is still in charge; *He* is the Lord of the harvest (Matthew 9:36-39).

One way to drive this point home is through our prayers. One simple exposure exercise is to ask students to write out prayers in response to the needs that they have heard about. Pointing students to passages related to prayer, missions, and responding to those in need, can help direct their efforts.

Writing to missionaries (perhaps including the prayers written for them) is another exposure device. It helps students personalize missions involvement, and it can also be a genuine encouragement to missionaries in other cultures. (It may even serve to change the missionaries' opinions of teenagers in America, of whom they usually hear only the worst.)

Invite missionaries to serve in the youth group. Although I have already warned against the misuses of missionaries in the youth group, some are excellent possibilities for membership in the youth leadership.

Our best exposure has come from those who were accepted missionary candidates who were working through the missionary-preparation process while they served on youth leadership staff. Allowing students to see their preparation, their fears, and their ultimate obedience to God has provided a very valuable education for our youth group members.

Interviews and panel discussions. Interviewing the senior pastor or the leader of the missions committee are both excellent ways to expose the youth group to what your church is doing and can do in missions.

A panel discussion—perhaps three to five missionaries—can help students see the variety of people that God calls into Christian ministry. Answering questions from their varied perspectives, these missionaries can help our students say to themselves, "Maybe God could use *me* like that!"

The Media. InterVarsity Missions,[10] the U.S. Center for World Missions,[11] and any number of missions organizations can point us to the videos, movies, and slide shows available on missions subjects. Some will be informational, and others will be testimonial. A balance of both is recommended in order to help keep the group both informed and inspired.

I strongly recommend that any media resource be screened before usage, however. Perhaps the youth leader and several reliable students should view the presentation in advance and decide if it is useful for the group. While there are some outstanding missions resources available in the media, there are also some real "bombs" that should be avoided.

Bible studies on missions themes. "Understanding Acts 1:8 Today" or "The Great Commission and You" are some of the most personal ways to help students understand God's call on their lives. A series in Acts, an examination of Psalm 96, or a study of God's call on Moses (Exodus 3–4) are all possibilities which can help students integrate the biblical themes with their own lives and expectations for the future.

Responding to world events. One idea which we have tried on occasion to increase concern about the world is called "News in Review."[12] This activity—using newspapers or news journals—gives students the opportunity to look over a variety of international

events and then decide what they think are the top priorities. As they do this, the leaders pose three questions:
- Do you think God is concerned about these events?
- Were you aware of these events when they happened?
- Were you concerned enough to pray?

Such an activity is useful in that it helps students start to be more aware of the integration of the world news and their prayers. If we can help students care enough to *pray* when they hear of coups, disasters, wars, and tragedies around the world, they will be well on their way to becoming world Christians.

It is important that we not overestimate our students' concern about the world. An effort to help our students respond to world events may yield a discovery that many are quite apathetic about the world beyond their touch. Our exposure efforts can be the remedial response, giving students a practical realization of the need to bring insurmountable concerns before the God who can act.[13]

If we are going to make "expanding our world view" a priority in our lives and ministries, we cannot just stand up at the youth fellowship meeting and state, "Missions is our priority." We must *show* that missions is our priority through the focus of the youth group, through our willingness to make missions learning part of the overall curriculum, and through teaching youth group members how to start responding.

Jesus taught that our mouths will be expressions of our top priorities, "For out of the overflow of the heart the mouth speaks" (Matthew 12:34). If we expect our students to be talking about missions, we need to place world-Christian learning at the heart of our ministries.

NOTES

[1]"Where in the World—A World Awareness Game" for ages eight and up is available from Aristoplay Ltd., P.O. Box 7645, Ann Arbor, MI 48107.

[2]For information, contact World Concern, Box 33000, Seattle, WA 98133.

[3]The "Underground Church" simulation can be helped by contacting an agency that specializes in work behind the Iron Curtain. Slavic Gospel Association (P.O. Box 1122, Wheaton, IL 60189), Romanian Missionary Society (P.O. Box 527, Wheaton, IL 60189), and Open Doors with Brother Andrew (P.O. Box 2510, Santa Ana, CA 92799) are some of the organizations which could help.

[4]Patrick Johnstone, *Operation World: A Handbook for World Intercession* (Bromley, England: STL Books, 1980).

[5]David B. Barrett, ed., *World Christian Encyclopedia* (New York: Oxford University Press, 1982).

[6]Contact World Vision (919 West Huntington Dr., Monrovia, CA 91016) for information.

[7]Contact Compassion International (P.O. Box 7000, Colorado Springs, CO 80933) for information.

[8]Tony Campolo's *Ideas for Social Action* (Grand Rapids, Michigan: Zondervan/Youth Specialties, 1983) has some great ideas under categories like "Service Projects that Meet Human Need," "Ways for Young People to Impact the Social System," and "Raising Funds for Social Action."

[9]"Sidewalk Sunday School" at the Wheaton Bible Church (Wheaton, Illinois) took students to housing projects in the neighboring town of Carol Stream where they worked with latchkey kids from white, black, Mexican, and Oriental families. See *Youthworker Journal* (Summer 1984, pp. 64–67) for a full explanation.

[10]InterVarsity Missions (Box 7895, Madison, WI 53707).

[11]The U.S. Center for World Missions (1605 East Elizabeth St., Pasadena, CA 91101).

[12]Taken from Paul Borthwick, "What in the World Is God Doing?" *Pacesetter (Vol. 7)—Give It Away!* (Elgin, Illinois: David C. Cook, 1987), p. 33.

[13]Paul Borthwick, *Any Old Time—Book 5* (Wheaton, Illinois: Scripture Press, 1986). This meeting manual contains ideas for missions exposure based on Acts 1:8. Four programs are oriented to instruct students about local outreach (Jerusalem); four others move out into the community (Judea); the next four involve students in reaching "outcasts" (Samaria); and the final four discuss our world missions responsibilities (the ends of the earth).

Sample Missions Quiz

Section 1: Multiple choice—circle the correct answer.

1. Ulan Bator is the capital of (a) Yugoslavia; (b) Argentina; (c) Mongolia; (d) U.S.A.
2. The largest group of unreached people in the world is (a) the Chinese; (b) the Muslims; (c) Race track goers in the United States; (d) Europeans.
3. The religion of Pakistan is (a) Hindu; (b) Buddhism; (c) Islam; (d) Episcopalian.
4. William Carey is (a) a missionary now serving in Bangladesh; (b) the "father of modern missions"; (c) a shortstop for the St. Louis Cardinals; (d) a member of Grace Chapel who is interested in missions.
5. Dr. J. Christy Wilson, a professor at Gordon-Conwell Seminary, is famous for (a) flunking Paul Borthwick; (b) passing Paul Borthwick; (c) knowing Paul Borthwick; (d) serving as a missionary in Afghanistan.
6. Mauritius is a country located in (a) Central Africa; (b) the Indian Ocean; (c) Asia; (d) southern South America.
7. A person who works in a secular job in a country which will not allow missionaries is called a (a) crazy suicidal maniac; (b) tentmaker; (c) self-supporting witness; (d) all of the above.
8. Paul and Christie Borthwick are hoping to serve/live someday in (a) Bermuda; (b) Zaire; (c) Hawaii; (d) China.
9. What is the capital city of Greenland? (a) Godthaab; (b) Reykjavík; (c) Oslo; (d) Gunnbjorn.

Section 2: True/False

_____ **10.** World population is one billion.
_____ **11.** Albania has a flourishing Christian church.
_____ **12.** Kinshasa is the capital of Zaire.
_____ **13.** Hong Kong will become part of the People's Republic of China in our lifetime.
_____ **14.** One of the great challenges of modern missions is organization.
_____ **15.** Slavery is no longer practiced anywhere in the world.

Section 3: Discussion Starters (Note: The leader may not want to use these statements as part of the quiz but in another part of the meeting to get people talking.)

Agree/Disagree: People who do not know Jesus Christ personally are going to hell.

Agree/Disagree: Every American is so wealthy by world standards that he/she must be involved in missions.

Agree/Disagree: Communism is the greatest threat to Christianity in the world.

Answers (1–15 only)
(1.) c; (2.) a; (3.) c; (4.) b; (5.) d; (6.) b; (7.) b; (8.) d; (9.) a; (10.) False: it is now over 5 billion; (11.) False: Albania is one of the most repressive countries with respect to the Christian church. There are few—if any—known Christians there. (12.) True; (13.) True, in 1997; (14.) True; (15.) False. There is still evidence of slavery in various countries of northern Africa.

Sample Missions Crossword

DOWN (Old Testament)
 1. He could have been a "missionary" but he failed.
 2. She acted and made it necessary to have missions.
 4. He was the one through whom "all nations of the earth would be blessed."
 5. She was a missionary to the Persian king.
 6. God told Israel to be a "light to the _____."
10. But God told Israel to reach out to the "_____ and strangers."
11. He was a missionary in Egypt.
12. The people of Israel were hesitant to "witness" to these people.

ACROSS (New Testament)
 1. All Christians are to be known by this quality.
 3. The greatest missionary in the Book of Acts.
 5. A Greek word which we translate the "nations."
 7. He failed on his first trip as a missionary.
 8. He was timid, but he became a missionary to Ephesus.
 9. All Christians are commanded to _____.
12. When we go, we bring the _____.
13. This is where Paul almost made it to before he was captured.
14. Nickname of the apostle who went to India, according to legend.
15. God does not want any to _____.

After students complete the puzzle, go over the correct answers: Down—(1) Lot; (2) Eve; (4) Abraham; (5) Esther; (6) nations; (10) aliens; (11) Joseph; (12) Gentiles. Across—(1) love; (3) Paul; (5) *ethne;* (7) Mark; (8) Timothy; (9) go; (12) Gospel; (13) Spain; (14) Tim; (15) perish.

Taken from: Paul Borthwick, *Any Old Time Book 5* (Wheaton, Illinois: Scripture Press, 1986), pp. 65–66.

"Your Opinion" Handout

This was prepared by the staff of the Emmanuel Gospel Center (2 San Juan Street, Boston, MA 02118) to help suburban students articulate their feelings and stereotypes about the inner city.

1. Take two minutes to list positive and negative characteristics of the city.
2. What kind of people live in the city?
3. The best way to achieve harmony between different racial and cultural groups is: (choose two)
   (1) to encourage tolerant attitudes
   (2) to integrate schools, housing, and jobs
   (3) through social activities such as sports, the arts, and literature
   (4) through mutual respect for one's worth and dignity
   (5) to redistribute the wealth
   (6) through education
4. The city has many elderly people because:
   (1) They like to be around other people.
   (2) There is public transportation so that they can get around.
   (3) They have no choice.
   (4) The city is their home.
   (5) There are a lot of social care services.
5. Most blacks live in the cities because:
   (1) They can't afford to live in the suburbs.
   (2) They don't like whites.
   (3) They like the city.
   (4) Whites won't let blacks live in their neighborhoods.

True or False
6. Most poor people don't have to stay poor.
7. From my experience blacks are not as intelligent as whites.
8. City churches usually will stay and minister to the neighborhood they are in when it undergoes some type of change such as economic or racial.
9. Statistics show that crime in the city is committed mostly by minority persons.

Comments
10. Do you think the city is a good place to live and raise a family? Why or why not?

CHAPTER TEN
EXPOSURE IN THE HOME

The impact that parents have on their children has already been discussed in chapter 5, but it bears some repeating here, if only to point out that an expanded world view in the students we work with is as much a result of missions-oriented parents as it is a result of our youth group emphasis.

Dr. Terry Hulbert, in his booklet *Discipling Leaders with a Vision for the World,* cites the excellent example of Dick Winchell, the General Director of TEAM (The Evangelical Alliance Mission). According to Hulbert, Dr. Winchell and his wife "prayed that they would not see their grandchildren until they were two or three years old, meaning that all their children would go to the field right after they were married, or would be married on the field."[1]

If the young people we work with are coming out of world-Christian homes, they cannot help but grow in their world views.

What the Home Communicates

Exposure to missions in the home might mean a subscription to *National Geographic,* a world map in the family room, or a meal-time reading and prayer that pertains to God at work in the world. These and many other tangible expressions of world concern can encourage students in the same direction.

But there is more that is communicated in the home. Through the use of time, money, and energy, parents communicate three lessons to their children.

First, parents can communicate *attitudes.* My friend Mark is now a missionary in Africa; but in his case, his obedience to God's call was in spite of the attitudes he learned from his parents. In spite of professed Christian faith, his parents communicated that people like missionaries and pastors were lazy folks who chose to "work for God" because they were afraid of "good, old-fashioned work."

Mark heard the call of God to go as a cross-cultural servant, but it was in spite of his family rather than because of their good influence. Dr. Terry Hulbert again cites the affect of the home:

> Attitudes need to be implanted in the home. If the parents have a concern for the lost and are praying the Lord of the harvest to send out reapers, it will have an effect on the other family members.[2]

Second, parents can communicate *values*. Debbie came from a home where missionaries were held up as the greatest people in the world. In her family, missionaries and others who brought the Scriptures to the "ends of the earth" (Acts 1:8) were held up as God's adventurers. To Debbie, nothing was better than the idea of becoming a missionary. No wonder she has entered college determined to pursue cross-cultural service!

Fred's family communicates an equally essential value for world-mindedness. His parents—by their outreach and evangelistic entertaining—have shown Fred the value of reaching out in love to people who do not know Jesus Christ. As a result, Fred has always been one of the leading proponents of evangelistic outreach in our youth ministry.

An article in the *Latin America Evangelist* underscored the importance of values communicated at home by pointing to young people who had experienced their first call to missionary service before the age of ten. In summarizing the article, missionary statesman Horace Fenton wrote, "I thoroughly believe children can be called at an early age. And it happens most frequently in a home where children have been surrounded by not only an emphasis on missions, but by a vital commitment [to Christ] on the part of the parents."[3]

In his book *A New Face for the Church*, Larry Richards makes this same point as he observes that "teens who respond to evangelism training to win others to Christ were in each case from homes where the parents are committed, witnessing Christians."[4]

Third, parents can communicate *aspirations*. At some point during a child's upbringing, parents communicate (directly or indirectly) their hopes for his or her life. In Debbie's case (above), her parents communicated their aspirations that she would serve Christ—maybe in another culture.

In this materialistic age, Debbie's parents are quite exceptional. Many young people are growing up with aspirations to "make money," "be secure," "go to the top," and "succeed." Many of these aspirations are the direct result of signals that are being communicated at home.

Randy is an extreme case, but his family points out the issue well. When he first started voicing his concern for people who were poorer, less-fortunate, and "lost," his parents let their aspirations for him be known. As he entered his senior year of high school, they told him, "If you decide to pursue this service thing of yours, that's up to you, but we will offer you support for school *only* if you decide to go into business."

Whatever Randy's goals are for himself with respect to serving God and others, he knows that his parents aspirations are quite different.

How Can We Help?

Providing missions exposure in the home is not our realm of responsibility as youth workers, but we can do our best to assist parents whenever we can. Some of the basic ways that we can encourage parents include:

Channel missions resources to them. Books, periodicals, and new ideas in helping families get interested in missions are extremely helpful to the parent who is trying to build world awareness at home.

Many mission agencies have pamphlets and collections of ideas on how to "missionize" the home. We can write for this information and provide it for interested families. The sample evaluation form from Overseas Crusades (at the end of this chapter) is one tool that we used to help parents in their efforts.[5]

Affirm their ministry. One way that we can encourage parents is to remind them of the long-term impact that they are having on their young people. This can come in one of two forms.

One type of affirmation is designed to support the frustrated, tired parent. In this case, we point out the fact that the values and attitudes of parents do in fact yield long-term results in the lives of students. Our efforts will bolster the confidence of weary parents who wonder, "Am I making *any* difference in the life of this fifteen-year-old?"

Another type of affirmation is for the careless Christian parent. In meetings with groups of parents who are nominal Christians (with little evidence of a daily walk with God), I have often encouraged them by stating, "I want you to know that you folks will indeed have the greatest long-term influence on your children."

At about the time I sense that they are getting excited about that fact, I add my challenge. "Therefore, I must remind you that I cannot take your young people further in their relationship with God than you have gone yourselves. If you are not witnessing to your friends, it will be very difficult to challenge your teenager to reach out. If you do not read the Bible daily, how can I expect your students to do so? If you do not care enough about God's work in the world to pray daily about it, how can we build young people to be world Christians?"

By about the third question, parents have heard my challenge: they may be the most influential, but they are also the most responsible.

Encourage the missions-minded to speak up. In every youth group, there are usually at least one or two families who are trying to communicate a healthy world vision in their homes. We can encourage this in each family if we get these positive-example families to share their ideas with others.

Encourage parents to serve. There are some opportunities that families can undertake together as service projects. If parents make family service a priority, the students will be positively affected.

Older teens, however, may not be open to serving alongside of Mom or Dad, so the best example that the parents can set is their own willingness to serve elsewhere.

The Roberts family illustrated this beautifully. The two high-school-age daughters wanted to serve on a summer mission team, but they saw it as more of a family effort because—as the two young women were going off in one direction to serve—their mother was leading another of our youth service teams, and their father was staying at home to take care of the rest of the family so that the threesome could go out in service. Even though they were not all serving together, they all saw service as a family venture.

While the family is not the only source of missions vision for young people, it is an essential part of the vision-expanding process. As a result, we must do our part to help parents grow as world Christians themselves so that their young people get sustained exposure to God's world which will help expand their world views.

NOTES

[1]Terry Hulbert, *Discipling Leaders with a Vision for the World* (Wheaton, Illinois: Association of Church Missions Committees, 1984), p. 8.

[2]*Ibid.*, p. 9.

[3]"Can Kids Get a Missionary Call?" *Latin America Evangelist* (January—March 1988), p. 15.

[4]Larry Richards, *A New Face for the Church* (Grand Rapids, Michigan: Zondervan, 1981), p. 29.

[5]The Association of Church Missions Committees (P.O. Box ACMC, Wheaton, Illinois, 60189) is also a great place to pursue ideas on "missionizing" the home.

SAMPLE EVALUATION FORM

For each statement circle the number under either A (Always), O (Often), So (Sometimes), Se (Seldom), or N (Never).

	A	O	So	Se	N
1. Our family prays together about the Lord leading us collectively & individually into missionary service.	5	4	3	2	1
2. Our family prays at least once per week for our church-supported missionaries.	5	4	3	2	1
3. Our family reads missions books together during our devotions.	5	4	3	2	1
4. Our family finds creative ways of supporting a missionary or missions project.	5	4	3	2	1
5. Our family corresponds with a missionary family overseas.	5	4	3	2	1
6. Our family entertains missionaries in our home whenever we get the chance.	5	4	3	2	1
7. Our family participates in our church's missions program and activities.	5	4	3	2	1
8. Our family gets together with new & old friends in the neighborhood with an outreach ministry in mind.	5	4	3	2	1
9. Our family takes field trips of different kinds to learn more about ethnic groups and foreign cultures.	5	4	3	2	1
10. Our family discusses world missions in relation to the current events reported in the news.	5	4	3	2	1

How do you rate? Add up your circled numbers and check your score.

10–20 It's time to pour new cement for your foundation.
21–30 Your foundation seems okay, but now you need to remodel your

interior.

31–40 Your house is in pretty good shape, but it still needs a few repairs.

41–50 Excellent condition! Now keep up with the upkeep!

Written by Conrad Wilcox. Reprinted by permission from *Team Horizons*, a publication of TEAM.

Section
Four

EXPANDING YOUR STUDENTS' WORLD VIEW
Basic Ingredient #3—Experiences in Missions

In our efforts to expand the world view of the high school or junior high students that we are working with, the good examples of section 2 have provided a model of world concern. The exposure to missions in section 3 has stimulated a missions mind-set in the home, youth group, or church.

Experiences in missions service, however, are perhaps the most critical element needed in expanding the world view of young people. These experiences show students that, in response to the great world and the awesome needs that they are becoming familiar with, they can make a difference!

Why Offer Experiences?

In the busy world of average youth leaders, more planning for experiences in service may not be a welcome idea. The schedule is so full already. Why add more to it?

The results in the lives of students are the most significant reason to make the time for these service opportunities in the life of the youth group. These results are more fully covered in chapter 20, but for now, consider the following observations.

Service projects get students' eyes off themselves. Joanie was one of the most insecure members of our youth group. A junior in high school, her self-consciousness was most evident in her constant preoccupation with her looks. When she came on a service team with us into a Third World location, I thought for sure that she would die from dirty hair and makeup withdrawal.

Over the course of three hard weeks of service, Joanie learned a very valuable lesson. She found that her acceptance on the team and before God was based on who she is, not how she looks. She still wears makeup and perms her hair, but her self-esteem is not so attached to these externals anymore. Serving others helped her get her eyes off herself.

A special section of one *Youthworker Journal* discussed the phenomenon they called "apathy-busting" in youth ministry. One of the best ways to break apathy in students, they said, was to get them out in service to others:

> The key to turning apathy into excitement is getting kids' focus off of themselves and onto others. When young people can discover their self-potential, and have opportunities to utilize that potential, their views about God, the Christian faith, and they themselves can be revolutionized.[1]

Service projects motivate students. Motivation is always a hot issue for youth leaders. How can we get students to take greater responsibility for themselves? How can we stir them to action?

In *A Guide for Motivating Youth*, the authors assert, "Church leaders who seek to motivate young people will need to provide experiences which expose them to needs and provide opportunities for the Holy Spirit to do His convicting work in their hearts."[2]

A successful experience of seeing God use her life on a mission team to Colombia motivated Michelle to start serving in her own neighborhood. She determined as a high school sophomore, "God has me here; there's not too much I can do about the lonely, hurting people I saw in the barrios of South America—at least now. But I can reach out to the hurting, lonely people at the nursing home in my neighborhood."

Michelle organized a program for our youth group called "Adopt-a-Granny" where high school students would go for two hours per week to visit with an adopted grandparent who was otherwise alone at the nursing home.

A service team experience for Don motivated him in another way. As a result of a cross-cultural team where he did evangelistic work, he came back to his senior year of high school determined: "If I can go all the way to Latin America to share Christ with people I've never met, I must go across the hall at school to reach students I've been in school with all of my life."

Service projects help students see that they can make a difference in the world. A conversation with one high school student left a lasting impression on me in terms of our need to help students make an impact on their world.

After what I thought was a good presentation on the hungry people of the world, this student approached me, obviously agitated.

He said, "How dare you make me feel guilty about these people that I can do nothing about. I have too many problems of my own. I don't care about hungry people!"

This was a leader in the youth group, a student that I would have held up as an example of discipleship in action. And he said he didn't care! Where had I gone wrong? How had I failed?

My failure was in the presentation of the vast, overwhelming statistics without any suggested responses. The student's frustration was not due to apathy; it was due to helpless feelings in the face of situations to which he wanted to respond.

Service projects, work days, and mission teams provide tangible practical ways for students to start making a difference in the world of need that we are presenting to them.

How Do We Do It?

Each youth group will want to consider what is most appropriate. Some groups will start with afternoon projects after school. Others may consider a weekend work project. Many are now looking into the one- or two-week service team, the model that we have found most effective in the past ten years at Grace Chapel.

Though there are no easy answers or "tips for success" which will apply to every youth group, there are at least three basic principles which every youth leader will want to keep in mind as he or she gets started and tries to decide the most appropriate service option for a particular youth group.

First, plan ahead. When a youth leader calls me in June trying to plan for an international, two-week missions trip for July, I know that he has vastly underestimated the task ahead. Long-term planning usually yields better long-term results and also helps keep the youth leader from losing his or her mind in the last-minute planning scramble.

Second, start small and build. In light of fact that international, cross-cultural teams are now quite possible, many youth leaders will want to "jump right in" and start with a big trip to a very faraway place.

One youth leader called me up for advice. He wanted to know if he was being too zealous in his first attempt. What was it? A six-week venture to Kenya! I graciously tried to tell him that I thought he was being a little too ambitious in the first effort.

It is far better to start with small, close-to-home teams, for shorter periods of time (and make these successful) than it is to attempt something very risky, only to have a failure nullify the possibility of future teams.

Third, pay attention to details. The incredible potential of these mission experiences can be altogether lost if the confusion of misplaced tickets, wrong connections, and poor health preoccupies the team. Attention to details is the best way to insure the learning environment of the team experience.[3]

What Will Make a Service Team Effective?

The next chapters will be dedicated to answering this question. The eight chapters that follow include the aspects of mission team planning which we have found to yield the greatest growth in lives of students.

These ideas were part of our first teams in 1978 (although many have been significantly expanded since then), and now, some 65 teams later, we believe in these ideas more than ever.

NOTES

[1]"Breaking Through the 'Me' Barrier—Programs to Expand Your Kids' World," *Youthworker Journal* (Summer 1985), p. 34.

[2]Diane Wheatley and Carol Bostrom, *A Guide for Motivating Youth* (Glendale, California: G/L Regal, 1977), p. 16.

[3]*How To Plan, Develop, and Lead a Youth Missionary Team* (Grace Chapel, 59 Worthen Road, Lexington, MA 02173) is a helpful booklet in identifying the details of organizing mission service teams.

CHAPTER ELEVEN
PREPARATION

Earlier in this book, I noted that our summer mission team program got started in 1978, but it was an experience a year later that taught us the need for thorough preparation for these service experiences.

The summer service team to an Indian reservation in Canada had successfully painted the buildings that they were assigned, but they alienated some of the missionaries in the process.

The missionaries' evaluation was blunt. "The students seemed more interested in pairing off with each other than in having significant contact with the Indian students. They also seemed more inclined to play than to work. If they had been prepared to work, we could have accomplished twice as much."

That team brought the flaws of our program to our attention so vividly that I determined that such a fiasco would never happen again.

Service experiences can be a vision-expanding tool in the youth ministry, but only if they are made up of leaders and students who are *prepared* to work. If young people go because it is the "thing to do"[1] or because of a desire for adventure (which is useful, but cannot be the primary motivation), the team may fail or, at best, will fall short of its potential to provoke growth.

The success of a service project, mission team, or even a work day is often determined before the van leaves the church parking lot or the plane takes off. The key is in the preparation of both leaders and students.

Whether students serve for a weekend or for a month, we err if we do not teach them that missionary work demands preparation. Students must learn that growth takes work; the bodybuilder Charles Atlas' phrase, "No pain, no gain" should be one that our students learn to apply to the Christian life.

Fund-raising, assignments, interviews, and other preparations all communicate to students a basic message: "We are taking this service project seriously, and if you desire to serve with us, you'll take it seriously too!"

What Type of Preparation?

The preparatory requirements must be varied according to the youth group, the project to be tackled, and the intensity of the cultural "jump"; but in general, it helps to modify the requirements according to the answers to five basic questions.

The first question is *how long?* An afternoon of leaf-raking at the home of an elderly person should not demand the same preparation as a week-long trip. We vary the requirements according to the amount of time that the project will take.

In the case of one-day projects into the city of Boston to work with some Haitian congregations, we require only that students show up on time, bring their lunches, and come ready to work. We require little in terms of team preparation or learning to work with others because the time of the project will not allow for a real team to form. We are, in this case, a group of independent workers who happen to be together for the day.

A two-week team experience in Haiti, however, is quite a different matter. In this case, we want to make sure that students know *how* to work (we can afford to send them to Boston to be lazy; we cannot afford to send them overseas to loaf) and how to work *together* (because in the overseas setting they become an interdependent team).

Question number two is *what task?* On one of our teams, we were traveling over 4,000 miles in order to paint a school building. We knew before we got there that our work was needed. The missionary had told us that our paint job could make the difference for the school regarding the government inspection which was coming up. A good paint job meant a passed inspection and the qualifications needed to stay in operation!

On this team, we had to make sure that our team members not only knew how to paint but paint well. In the preparation process, we required that team members all attend a Saturday morning seminar where a professional painting contractor gave us three hours of instruction and practice rolling, "cutting in," and doing trim.

In this case, the task defined the preparation needed. (Incidentally, the school passed the government inspection!)

Question number three: *Where?* Cross-cultural training will obviously vary according to the destination of a service team. The "things to bring" lists, training regarding keeping healthy, and the fund-raising preparation will all be affected by the destination.

We have had weekend teams that did all of their preparation on the Friday night before they went out. In the case of one of our most difficult teams, an evangelism team to France and Spain, the training occurred over the course of almost six months.

Question number four: *How much?* It may sound crassly material-istic to increase the amount of preparation in proportion to the cost of the project, but it is a statement to team members and supporters that greater expense means greater responsibility.

Students are more likely to get financial supporters as the cost of a service experience goes up. If this is the case, we want students to understand that we need to be that much more prepared because we are responsible to the people who are investing in us and in our ministry.

Question five is *what other opportunities will the team be afford-ed?* Preparation must also be determined according to the experi-ences that the team can anticipate. If students will go through the poorest areas of our own country, they will be more able to respond if they have been prepared by reading or understanding some of the causes of poverty.

Teams that will have the opportunity to speak in churches may want to get musical or how-to-give-your-testimony training. If there will be exposure on the trip to other world religions (like Islam or Hinduism), the team will benefit by preparation which includes a basic understanding of the tenets of these religions.

After determining the intensity of the mission experience that lies ahead, we can then decide on what type and amount of preparation is warranted. In general, the preparatory requirements fall into three categories:[2] personal preparation, team preparation, and pa-rental preparation.

Personal Preparation

One of the greatest side effects of these mission experiences is that students begin to understand what it means to take responsibility for their own lives. This effect is enhanced when there are require-ments that help students be personally prepared.

One requirement is *applications.* Assuming that the trip will be longer than a few days, the application process should help students get the message that a missions team is not just a "Y'all come!" type of activity. They will see from the outset that this is serious business.

In our application process, we started by asking two questions: "How do you know that you are a Christian?" and "Why do you want to serve on this team?" The answers to these gave us a basic understanding of the faith and the motivation of the student.

Over the years, we have added questions like, "What strengths or weaknesses do you bring to this team?" or "Give the names of two fellow students who can attest to your Christian witness at high school."

Another requirement could be *writing assignments*. Reports on the area of the country of the world to which the team will go, book reports, or reports on the type of service being performed (curriculum research for a Vacation Bible School project, etc.) are all helpful in seeing if students can discipline themselves to carry out assignments. This foreshadows their ability to take responsibility on the team.

Fund-raising is a third possible requirement. According to the youth group, the traditions of the church, or the economic means of the students, the financial preparation can take on a variety of forms. Some will choose fund-raisers (an excellent way to involve the *entire* youth group in a project, even those who will not serve on the mission team). Others may look for work days for team members so that they can raise the monies needed through efforts in the community.

We have chosen to require that our students be totally responsible for their own funding. We tell them the cost of the project as early as possible so that they can save, ask for monetary gifts at Christmas, or start praying. They are then allowed to apply to the Missions Committee (which requires another two page form, a book report, and an interview with the Committee). We also offer them training on how to write "prayer-supporter" letters as they raise their needed finances.

Requiring students to raise their own funds has served as one of the greatest faith-enhancers of our trips. Over the years, students have grown as they saw God provide the money that they needed in some miraculous ways!

One student needed to raise $600. She applied to our Missions Committee, wrote supporter letters, and contacted others to join her in prayer. Before her trip was ready to depart, she returned $160 to the missions budget because God had provided her with more money than she needed. She wanted to help some of the other students with her excess!

Another requirement is *prayer*. The fund-raising often leads to growth in faith as students learn to commit their needs to the Lord and trust Him to provide as they need it. To encourage further growth in prayer, we also require that students raise three prayer supporters to intercede on their behalf before, during, and after the service team experience.

Prayer letters, mandatory attendance at the church prayer meeting, or prayer support for other team members can all be part of the faith-building aspect of preparation.

A final requirement can be *writing*. Although we have not always been successful, we do try to require students to start a spiritual journal before their mission team experience and to maintain it during the trip. (We call them spiritual journals because very few students keep "diaries" anymore.)

To foster this writing, we do offer training—a one-page instructional sheet on "How to Write in Your Journal"—but not every student responds as we would like. Our hope is that students will be able to map their own growth throughout the preparation and service experience.

Team Preparation

The discipleship that can take place in the midst of a service team experience is usually a direct result of relational growth that occurs on the team. In addition to the spiritual dimension, however, the preparation of the team is critically important because these mission experiences usually involve diverse people working in new surroundings in potentially stressful conditions where interdependence is mandatory.

All of these elements work together to intensify the need for the team to be prepared together. One training tool we have used is *a team training retreat.*[3] A full weekend away together, in a situation that is relatively controlled, gives us the best possible environment for building our team into a cohesive unit. Meals together, shared lodging, hard work, and stress-activities (like scaling a twelve-foot wall, using the "trust fall" and other obstacle-course activities) all simulate the experiences of the work-team that lie ahead.

Our experiences with these team retreats have taught us some critically important lessons in the preparation for mission service teams. We have learned that:

• Students who refuse to cooperate on the retreat are usually obnoxious on the service team.

• Lazy students—if not confronted—behave the same way on the retreat as they will on the trip.

• Those who cannot control their romantic desires on a retreat (i.e., he or she must have a retreat weekend "steady") will almost always be divisive in the team experience.

In other words, we have learned to watch the team behavior on the retreat closely because what we see there is a foreshadowing of things to come on the mission team. In most cases, we have helped our teams grow by confronting the problems we observed after the retreat (or on the retreat) but *before* the trip. In the most drastic cases, we have had to dismiss a team member after the retreat because he or she showed an unwillingness to respond to correction.

Another excellent training tool is *teamwork.* The criticism that will come most frequently with respect to international teams will sound something like, "Why can't you help meet the needs right here at home?"

The best response is to utilize the preparation phase of international teams in order to accomplish work here at home. In our preparatory phase for mission teams, team members have:

• spread wood chips in the gardens around our church grounds,

• painted buildings in some needy areas of Boston,

• helped a man reconstruct his garage so as to be a storage area for missionary supplies,

• and even helped elderly people plant their summer gardens.

Teamwork before the actual project both binds team members together and builds team confidence as small projects are successfully completed. These work projects beforehand are also wonderful opportunities for leaders to observe the team in action: Who are the "bossy" ones? Who are the hard workers? And who are the ones who really want to work but whose attention spans are so limited that jobs never seem to get completed?

Following the example of many discipleship programs, we have used a *team covenant* to help define the teams' activities and expectations. Our covenants have four sections—vision, goals, structure, and accountability.

The team *vision* defines the goals: What kind of family do team members want to be together? The team *goals* outline some of the qualities needed to reach that vision. This might include statements about forgiveness, Christlikeness, and servanthood.

The third covenant section, the team *structure,* is the most specific. This section outlines aspects of team behavior where the goals will be worked out. Team meetings, personal commitment to prayer or Bible study, or a definition of leadership on the team could all be part of the *structure* section.

The final section deals with *accountability* (or sometimes we call this *evaluation*). These are the statements that establish the criteria of how the team will know if the vision was accomplished.

We instituted the use of a team covenant in 1983, and we have never looked back. This statement, created by the team on the training retreat, has been the best part of our entire training process to help teens grow as individuals and as teams.

Team meetings are another useful training tool. Basic to any pre- paratory process are the times when the team members come together to exchange prayer requests, ask questions, and be given information pertinent to the team. The basic rule of thumb regard- ing team meetings is this: plan as many team meetings as needed to communicate the vital information and to keep the team morale positive.

The more complicated the team, the more information there is to communicate. For this reason, a standardized *team training manual* is most helpful. It serves as a way to consolidate information so that we, as leaders, can be *sure* that students have it.

A training manual also carries with it a subtle message which affirms students in their efforts. It says to them, their peers, and their parents that the training for this mission team is as important as orientation to a course or new job. "We're getting trained!"[4]

One of the greatest messages that the church can send to a youth mission team is, "We are proud of you; we're behind you!" An *official team send-off* (in a regular or a special service) is part of the team's training which bonds them to the church at large. It commu- nicates a sense of team pride as well as team responsibility because it reminds students that they go as representatives of Jesus Christ, the youth group, and the whole church.

Parental Preparation

Over the past few years, I have realized that a successful mission experience implies the partnership and participation of the parents. The effect of the home, both before or after the trip, is essential in building the world view of our students.

Good preparation for the parents is a little harder to quantify, but it definitely implies at least three things:

• *Communication.* Bill joined his summer team before his parents knew about it. Our systems at the youth group were inefficient in communicating with parents, so Bill was able to sign up and get

accepted onto a team before he told his parents that he was apply-
ing. Bill's parents were rightfully upset about our lack of
communication.

To prevent this oversight from occurring, we now incorporate the
parents into at least one of the team preparation meetings. This is
the best way to insure that the parents get accurate information,
understand the goals of the team, and realize their part in building
the missions vision of their son or daughter.

• *Prayer.* If the teams are going to be blessed and protected by
God, we must incorporate the intercessory prayers of concerned
parents. They will be the people most likely to pray every day for
the team, so we owe it to them to relate prayer requests and needs
as the team prepares and then goes.

One of our teams to Africa experienced three weeks with few
problems, very little sickness, and one wonderful cross-cultural experience after another. More than half of those team members are
now in Christian ministry or preparing for it. This team was also the
team which was supported most fervently by the parents in prayer.
Each parent was committed to daily prayer on our behalf, and the
team members benefited from God's answers to their faithfulness.

• *Involvement.* Many parents will struggle with letting their children go away from home for a service team. While this "letting go"
process is part of their child's maturation, we do not need to aggra-
vate the pain of parents by making them feel left out. We can recruit
their help, involve them in team meetings, and ask for their help in
the preparation process. It is imperative that we help young people
understand that their parents are partners with us in the sending
process.

Build a Strong Foundation

Service or mission team experiences are tremendous educational
tools for building the world vision of students and leaders alike, but
the foundational ingredient to these experiences must be
preparation.

Unprepared teams usually yield disillusioned students and frustrated leaders, not to mention irritated missionary host groups.
Good results in the lives of students and in families will be the result
of thorough planning and preparation.

In our youth ministry, we have intensified the requirements almost every year, and this has reaped very positive results, but it has
not been without its problems. Besides the logistical problems of

organizing all of the details, there are always a few students who refuse to do the required work or a few parents who want their teenager exempted from a particular requirement.

When one student told me that he could not attend the training retreat, I replied, "Well, we can't send you on a project this year. Maybe you can apply next year and plan on being on the retreat."

He was furious and pouted for several weeks about how unfair the church was. He complained to his mother, and she actively lobbied to try to get the decision reversed. Finally, I explained to the young man that his response to the decision pointed out that he lacked the spiritual qualifications to go on the team.

He reacted angrily again, but eventually cooled down enough to see that he was in need of growth. He dedicated himself to a discipleship group that next year, and went on a team the following summer.

There will be hassles with increased preparation, but the rewards far exceed the difficulties. Tough requirements and training have drawn out the best in our teenagers, and they have made the most of their service experiences.

NOTES

[1]Our experiences at Grace Chapel have created a situation where high school students have come to see youth mission teams as a "norm" rather than a special experience in serving. Comments like, "This team wasn't as good as last year's," or "Where are *you* going this year?" have shown us the dangers of mission teams becoming a "popular" part of the youth group. As a result, Tim Conder, our youth minister, has helped increase the requirements, using ongoing service as well as discipleship group commitment as criteria in the preparatory process. This sense of year-round preparation diminishes the fad involvement significantly.

[2]Some of the ideas and categories of this section appeared originally in *Leadership* magazine under the title, "Training Young People to Serve" (Fall 1984, pp. 91–92).

[3]Many of our concepts for the training retreat weekend should be attributed to the "Boot Camp" idea used by Teen Missions International in their program for training and preparing teenage summer missionaries.

[4]For youth leaders who are interested in a sample training manual, the Grace Chapel Youth Ministry sells copies of the team leader training manual (the youth manual plus some instructions for leaders). For information, write to "Super Summer Mission Teams," c/o Grace Chapel, 59 Worthen Road, Lexington, Massachusetts 02173.

CHAPTER TWELVE
TEAMWORK

The preparation process has made many of the provisions needed to foster teamwork, but there are other aspects of mission team experiences which can develop the group as a team.

We start by observing one basic truth about human nature: people will not blend together as a team unless *we plan for it* and *build toward it* as a goal. Selfishness, cliques, and isolation are the results of sin, and we must work against the ill effects of these relational realities in the youth teams that we take out.

As a contrast to the negative aspects of sinfulness, I should add that team work is also one of the greatest tools for youth discipleship. As we build team members together, and as we work in a service experience toward a common goal, we are able to exemplify the body of Christ in an unparalleled way.

Teamwork—before, during, and after a service project—also teaches one of the most important lessons of the Christian life: loving the people we do not like. If, as some missionaries assert, the greatest problem on the mission field is with relational breakdown between missionaries, then it is integrally important that we teach young people the truth of "loving even when you don't like" *before* they go out in full-time service.

We try to make this point on our training retreat, the first chance that team members have to see how different they really are. The student who dominates the one mirror in the cabin will make enemies quickly. The student who is always feigning injury or sickness to get out of work will be spotted and singled out by other team members. The unpopular student ("nerd," "geek," or other such name) will be laughed at and ridiculed. Where will these students experience love?

These are the opportunities we must take to teach that biblical love is not limited to our feelings or to the other person's desirability. Instead, it is an action that we take to demonstrate kindness or mercy. While we were undesirable sinners, Christ died for us (Romans 5:8). This is the type of love that will break down relational barriers and enable our teams to function as units.

Building for Teamwork—Before the Experience

The preparation phase provides ample opportunity for team leaders to see the team in action and to get a view of the relational strengths and weaknesses of their team before going out in service. But who is preparing the leaders? Effective experiences in service teams occur when the leaders also are as well-trained as possible.

In our structure, we try to start preparing the leaders at least two months before the preparation of the students begins. This gives our leaders time to prepare themselves in a variety of capacities.

1. They learn to work together. If there is more than one leader on a team, then the preparation of the "miniteam" of the leaders will be essential for team unity. On one of our South American teams, the "organizational" leader (our detail-oriented person) did not get along with our "relational" leader (the person who was prone to overlook details in favor of building better friendships). The whole team suffered until these two started functioning as a team.

It is best to get the leaders involved early so that they can understand their own personal strengths and weaknesses in an effort to provide excellent leadership to the team.

2. They can do needed research. Talking with other leaders who have coordinated teams in the past gives our present leaders the opportunity to build on the strengths (and avoid the failures) of past teams.

Training the leaders can also help the overall preparation because leaders can present the team with the questions already answered.

A few years ago, an article appeared in *National Geographic* on the effect of the tsetse fly in West Africa. In light of this, the leader of the team that was headed in that direction knew what questions students (and parents!) would be asking. A few calls to the mission station and the mission headquarters gave complete answers that added credibility to the leader and enthusiasm to the team.

3. They can learn what has worked. Good team leaders will want to know what activities, games, and events can help foster team unity. Advance preparation of leaders enables the leaders to talk with each other as well as with youth leaders so that team-building exercises can be planned before the leaders are swamped with a myriad of details.

4. They can learn to pace their team. Much of our training takes place from April to June, but some of our teams do not leave until late August. Advance preparation helps leaders know how to pace their team for maximum teamwork at the time of their departure.

We have sent two teams to Trinidad in the late-August time slot. The leaders of these two teams worked hard to build team momentum during the "lag" time through smaller service projects as well as frequent team meetings throughout the summer.

Building for Teamwork—During the Team Experience

An enthusiastic team retreat, followed by a host of meetings, and completed with a special service of commissioning from the church body will set a great pace for teamwork on the project, but it does not *guarantee* it! Other factors must be taken into account to help the team work well together and grow as interdependent members of one unit.

First, the leaders must lead. This sounds redundant, but it is totally possible for those who have been given leadership responsibility to abdicate leadership in favor of having the acceptance of team members.

Our experiences have taught us to reiterate to leaders one basic theme: It is more important to lead than it is to be liked! This means that leaders must, at times, make the unpopular decision if they perceive it is the best for the team.

There was a student on one of the teams that my wife and I led together who was getting quite disruptive to our team unity and teamwork. Her complaints about the foreign food, her whining about the hard, physical labor, and her pouting about the multiple church services we were involved in was hurting everyone.

My wife was given the task of confronting this young woman. The confrontation was not too pleasant. My wife went through the feelings every youth leader has in the face of confrontation: "What if I am being unfair?" "What if she turns the team against me?" "What if she won't talk to me for the remainder of our time here?"

Nevertheless, the confrontation occurred, and the student responded first with tears and more pouting, but then she came to the point of growth. At the end of the team project she was recognized as the "most improved worker."

Leadership requires a determination to act out of love, even if it means an uncomfortable confrontation or an unpopular decision. (Every youth worker knows how powerful his or her need for love from the students is, and this need must be overridden if proper leadership is to occur.)

Second, leaders must maintain their positions as pacesetters and examples. We encourage our leaders on two-week service projects to always be the hardest workers and to volunteer for the most difficult (or boring) jobs. This type of leadership—"I will not ask you to do anything that I will not do myself"—keeps team morale high.

We saw the opposite of this occur on one team led by a person in Christian ministry. Unfortunately, his stated desire to go to the mission field to "encourage missionaries" did not seem to be a potential problem, but it was. When the team, who had been assigned to paint a Bible school, arrived, the team leader (my pastor friend) made sure that the work was delegated to others in the first two days, and then he was off to "encourage missionaries." He did build some great relationships with the local workers, but he alienated his team. After a week of painting under the hot, equatorial sun, the team was demoralized because they saw their leader out having fun with the missionaries while they were stuck with the "dog work."

Third, the team vision must be communicated to the host. We try to accelerate this process by increased communication before we arrive, but it still must be stated at the work location.

One of our teams went to Mexico to build, and doing an excellent job was a team priority. The missionary host did not fully understand this. When he came back to the work site after leaving the team alone for four days, he told them that their work was all wrong and needed to be redone. The team was tired already, and this almost broke their spirits; they felt like failures.

If the host had known how much they wanted to do a great job, perhaps he would have stayed with them to make sure they were doing the job correctly at the outset.

In another missions setting, the host saw our team as more of a "tour group" than a "work team." At first, the team enjoyed the leisurely schedule, but then they started to ask, "Is this all we are going to do? We came here to *work*, not play!" The host had the wrong idea about why our group had come, and the students were feeling useless as a result.

Finally, encourage the team members to work together. One of our reasons for undertaking so many painting, general maintenance, and physical labor projects has been our desire for students to work as a team. Doing a job in close proximity to each other enables us to:

• encourage those who are getting discouraged with monotonous tasks,

• challenge the lazy,

• make sure the correct work is getting done,
• talk together about the service project and the experiences we are sharing,
• exemplify hard work to those with short attention spans,
• undertake jobs that make our students a success in serving (without doing harm to the work established by the local people),
• and affirm each other as we work.

In some settings, sending individuals or groups off to serve at some other location will be inevitable, but it is not the ideal that we would choose.

Building for Teamwork: After the Team Experience

Many of the activities that leaders can initiate to foster the team camaraderie after the project are covered in chapter 19 (Follow-up). There is, however, one event that leaders should plan in order to complete the team experience: a team reunion.

After one to three weeks of intense experience as a team, the team members will separate to their homes. In many cases, loneliness and even depression can result from the abrupt change. To help students debrief back into their normal lives, we plan a team reunion within one week of our return.

At a team reunion, we do any (and sometimes all) of the following:
• Look through *all* of the slides. We do this because we alone will appreciate what all of the pictures, places, and people really mean.
• Go over our journals to discuss what we learned.
• Talk about the hardships of returning, including the isolation some feel at home, the frustration of communicating intense experiences, or the loneliness some will feel for the people with whom we served.
• Sing songs or make jokes that mean something to us as a team.
• Pray together for God's grace to help us readjust to our present surroundings and yet not return to the same old lifestyle. We encourage each other to make changes as a result of our team experience.

The team reunion is also the best place to state that the team experience is one that should be treasured but will never be repeated. Our prayer is that our students will change as a result of the team experiences, but we realize that the two weeks will never be reconstructed. We want students to grow in the present.

CHAPTER THIRTEEN
EXPOSURE TO MISSIONARIES

The goal of our mission team experiences is to expand the world views of the students with whom we are working. With this goal in mind, our missions experiences must include our best efforts to show them the people that God is using in a variety of settings in our world.

Exposure to Christian workers (both locally and cross-culturally) communicates the message to our students that serving means sacrificial living. Bruce and Cherith had a healthy income, a nice suburban home, and a comfortable life, but God called them out of their comfort into service in Quito, Ecuador. They do love their new place of living and serving, but obedience to the Lord's call has been costly. The missions team that worked with them understands a little bit more about intentional sacrifice for the sake of obedience as a result of their work with Bruce and Cherith.

We take our young people into the "ghettos" of our country where they see godly men and women in action—even at the risk of their own possessions and safety. We introduce our young people to cross-cultural workers whose work among tribal peoples in the jungle exposes them to rare tropical diseases which could possibly shorten their life spans.

Exposure to missionaries can show students the sacrifices involved in obedience, but it can also show them the rewards of lives submitted to God. Many of the missionaries we have served alongside of *genuinely enjoy* what they are doing.

Bob and Helen, two of the missionaries who hosted a team that we sent, love the country, the people, and the ministry into which God has sent them. Jean—a missionary with over twenty-five years of ministry in Colombia—loves her place of service; all of her best friends are Colombian coworkers.

When we present the picture to young people that missionaries are those who obeyed (against their will, better judgment, and desires) by going to a faraway place, we may be overlooking God's activity in the desires of many missionaries. While there is sacrifice involved in any type of service to others, there are many missionaries who love their work, are strongly bonded to the people around them as partners and friends, and could not think of doing anything else. These are the people who have found their delight in doing the will of God (Psalm 42:8).

In our desire to present a balanced perspective to our young people, we must remember to introduce them to missionaries who are enjoying their obedience. There are many missionaries who are.

Proper exposure to missionaries in a service-team experience should provide a picture of balance—the sacrifice and the joy—for there is both in following Jesus Christ.

Planning for Good Exposure to Missionaries

Our teams have had both good and bad experiences in their exposure to the local workers and their missionary hosts. Some have met missionaries who adopted our team as part of their own family; others have worked for missionaries who scarcely talked to the team except to get them started working. Not every experience is wonderful, but this in itself is presenting a genuine view of missions to our young people, because not every missionary is cooperative, friendly, or loving.

There are some actions that we, as team planners and leaders, can take to facilitate the best possible growth in our team members through their exposure to the missionaries.

The first action falls under the category of *work*. The best teams we have ever sent out have been those that worked alongside the missionaries (and the local workers, where possible). Sustained exposure to these missionaries in a variety of contexts has enabled team members to see missionaries as "real people." The result has been deeper love and respect for these true partners in ministry.

On one team in West Germany, our foreman was a Dutch Christian who had offered his services to the camp. As a result of 15 hard days of work together, we gained a greater understanding of the challenges that Christians face in northern Europe (and we think that he had some of his stereotypes about Americans dispelled).

Bob and Helen, the missionaries referred to earlier, were willing to work with us throughout our three-week trip, in spite of the fact that they were both past retirement age. Their love for us was communicated through their partnership, and this encouraged the entire team.

Two of our Costa Rican teams experienced the contrast of missionaries by working alongside two very different men. One was a hard worker who saw himself as a co-laborer; he really understood American teenagers and took time to explain Costa Rican culture to the youth. The other man was more of a "boss" than a worker, and he desired that the work get done, regardless of whether or not the students learned anything about Costa Rica.

The co-laborer attracted students to missionary work; the "boss" turned the students off.

Working alongside the missionaries allows for growth in the students in a myriad of ways:

• They get to see missionaries as people just like themselves (even as sinners).

• They get to hear many of the "war stories" missionaries tell about their experiences over the years.

• They get to appreciate the work they are doing more because the missionary host communicates to them how important their labors are.

• They establish a personal friendship with a missionary with whom they can stay in touch after the trip is over.

Some of our best experiences in other cultures have included work alongside nationals in addition to the missionaries. This opportunity teaches students about nonverbal communication and about working as servants with the national church. It also is an excellent way for the local people to get to know our team members.

Meals are a second setting for growth. Eating is a human institution that communicates many cultural traditions and values. When these meals can be shared with missionaries, the whole team benefits from their educational explanations. The missionaries often reveal to us not only the significance of the meal or the custom; they also can give us instructions on how to eat properly in that culture.

One of our missionary hosts took us to a church in Naivasha, Kenya where the local church people provided us with a wonderful feast. In addition to serving as the translator, our host also gave us instructions on how to eat with the piece of bread we were given in place of utensils.

I was personally glad that he was there when the pastor came out with the specially roasted fish that had been prepared for our feast. As the leader of the group, I was given the place of honor—the head (eyes, brain, teeth, and gills included!) was reserved for me. Fortunately, our missionary host was older than I, and I deferred to him. In light of his greater age, he was more deserving of the honor. He relished the treat!

Meals together make our teams part of that missionary's family, and this again opens lines of communication between missionaries and students. It has been through conversations over the table where many of our students have learned the most about what missionary life is *really* like.

Fellowship and worship can also contribute to growth. Mike, our missionary host to five different teams since 1982, helps our teams get accustomed to cultural differences in West Germany by allowing our teams to participate in worship services with him. A native German, Mike can simultaneously explain the worship to us even as he explains our team to the people in the service.

Fellowship meetings and worship services with missionaries and the local people help our students realize many new things about the body of Christ:

• They may discover that God is worshiped in many languages, not just English.

• They often grow by worshiping with true "veterans" of the faith who have a deeper knowledge of God and a greater understanding of what it means to "take up their crosses" in following Christ.

• They learn the love of the local people as they are welcomed into the Christian fellowship, in spite of their differences.

• They hear of the power of God as people share their testimonies.

• They get a greater feeling of partnership with missionaries and local Christians as they share in prayer for each other.

The missionary host on one of our teams to Surinam, South America, arranged for us to have a worship service with a Surinamese youth group. There were linguistic barriers and some awkward moments at first, but as we sang songs together and listened to the teaching of God's Word, the barriers were lowered. The speaker gave a message to all of the young people on dating in a way that pleased God. In spite of the cultural differences, the young people were bound together as they learned about an issue that concerned them all.

Don't forget the importance of *having fun together*. Glen was perhaps the most adventuresome missionary that has ever hosted one of our teams. We visited him in Surinam on the fringes of the Amazon rain forest in northeastern South America. In the course of our two weeks with him, he took us alligator (cayman) hunting, piranha fishing, and for a little "jungle hike" (where we trudged through swampy water up to our waists).

It was the free time with Glen that left the most lasting impression on our students. His zest for life and reckless abandon in trusting God in every circumstance helped our students to be inspired by his example.

Not every missionary host is as adventuresome as Glen. Jean, the veteran missionary from Colombia, inspired our team through her willingness to address her fears. We took her snorkeling with us off the coast of Cartagena on our day off. She had never gone snorkelling in her 45-plus years of life, but, in spite of her fears, she gave it a try. After swallowing a gallon or so of the Caribbean, she started to get the hang of it. Her courage to try was what affected our team.

Free time with missionaries is an important part of the team because it gives students the chance to see that missionary life is also enjoyable. Very few missionaries live lives of complete suffering. In almost every area of the world, there are things to enjoy.

Creating the Learning Environment

Many of the young people we bring on service teams will be reticent to ask good questions of our missionary hosts. If they are courageous enough to speak, they may not ask the best questions pertaining to missionary work, and the opportunity to learn can be lost. As a result, it is best if leaders have some "primer" questions to ask when the team has time to listen to the missionaries. Here are a few samples:
• How did you become a Christian?
• How did God call you into missionary work?
• How did you know that God was calling you to this location?
• What have been the greatest sacrifices you have faced as a missionary?
• What have been your greatest rewards in your time of service?
• Do you have any regrets about coming here?
• What should we know about the local culture so that we do not offend anyone?
• What should we know about the worship service in terms of how it will differ from ours?
• In what ways have you seen God's Spirit at work here?
• Where could people like us "fit" in Christian ministry here?

As a result of numerous questions and long discussions with missionaries on our work teams, we have had students return to the service site as short-term missionaries, learn about the variety of ways that God calls people, and have their vision of God expanded.

Missionary answers to these and other questions have revealed:
- that demons and spirits are alive today, but God is still more powerful,
- that some missionaries are genuinely training the local people to take over the ministry, but others act as if they "own" the ministry,
- that God answers prayer in some bizarre ways,
- that hardships are part of following Christ and not necessarily a result of some sin,
- that love for God and His Word are primary requisites for missionary work—wherever we go!

Many of our students have at first felt uncomfortable asking questions, but as soon as they get to know the host, the questions begin to flow. We have seen these missionaries become "aunts," "uncles," and surrogate parents to the students on our teams.

Dave, Jim, and Sara have all been excellent examples of the impact that missionaries can have on the members of these service teams. Their effect on students has had little to do with the work actually accomplished by the team. Their impact has been a personal one; they saw the discipling of these students as part of their role as hosts.

In each case, these missionaries hosted students in their homes, made time to work with the team, and devoted two full weeks to serving alongside the group. I am sure that their own work suffered, but, as Dave stated to me, "We are investing in the lives of students who may join us here in service."

The best way to make sure that students benefit from exposure to missionaries is to communicate our expectations to the hosts *before* the work project. We send the names of team members to our hosts before the teams go in order to encourage the missionaries to be praying for these students by name. Through communication, the missionary hosts can see their greater role in being disciplers and influencers of students. If missionaries get this vision, the team members will all benefit.

CHAPTER FOURTEEN
EXPOSURE TO NEW CULTURES

When Liz attended her team's training meeting, she listened to the instructions being given about going through customs and baggage inspection in other countries. She was puzzled, so she raised her hand with a question:

"Why do we have to open our bags for these inspectors?" she asked.

"It is the normal rule," the leader replied.

"But I don't understand," Liz continued. "What *right* do they have to require me to open up my baggage?"

The leader finally understood the question. Liz was demonstrating that she had a very American view of the world, where "rights" and privileges were exercised.

The leader answered her honestly, "They have the right because it is *their* country, and they make the rules."

Liz was still flustered because, as an American, she thought she should have the freedom to travel the world at will without any infringement on her privacy. She had a difficult time accepting the fact that it was *their* country and not subservient to hers.

Expanding the world views of students includes sensitizing them to the fact that cultures and people are different. It also means helping them start to understand what it means to serve "cross-culturally," leaving the familiar behind in an effort to serve the Lord.

In every short-term service experience, there will be some aspect of "cross-cultural adaptation." Music, language, customs, clothing, and other things that we associate with "culture" will be different, even when we take service teams to other locations in the United States or Canada.

In general, training students with respect to culture should aim at three goals:

First, we want to instruct students that cultures can be different without being wrong. People in British countries do not drive on the "wrong" side of the road; they drive on the left. (If we want to find out what "wrong" is there, we should trying driving on the right!)

Second, we want to help students destroy stereotypes that they might hold about other peoples and cultures. The idea that "people are poor because they do not work hard" or "all people in the Third World are poor" can best be destroyed by healthy involvement in another culture. When students see people who work tirelessly in a market system that does not reward hard work, or when they see people in Third World countries whose generosity and love for people is "richer" than anything they have ever experienced, stereotypes are destroyed.

Third, we want to teach students that the rest of the world is not a "subsidiary of the United States." Of all the countries on earth, we Americans have a tendency to be the proudest and most provincial. Liz's question, "What right do they have?" indicates her basic assumption that all other nations should honor us because we are from the United States. By exposure to other cultures, we learn that we are *partners*, not masters, in our "global village."

Building Cross-cultural Appreciation

When we go to another culture, we are the strange ones. We are the ones with the unusual customs and unacceptable habits. We have the funny accents, the weird clothing, and the foreign perspectives. As ambassadors of Christ, we must realize that we are the guests in someone else's culture. We offer our respect, and we seek to learn so that we can get a greater view of our God's world.

With these realities in mind, then, what are some ways that we can build healthy cross-cultural appreciation into mission-team experiences?

First, spend time with the local people. In all our summer mission-teams experiences, the best cultural learning has taken place through exposure to and fellowship with the local people. On a trip to Appalachia, we try to help students meet those who have worked in coal mines or others whose families have lived "on the mountain" for five generations.

In foreign cultures, we send our students into the marketplaces and neighborhoods (with training and precautions, of course) so that they will be immersed in the day-to-day lives of the people we are serving.

Cultural exposure is not always easy, especially if there are teen-agers on our teams who cannot really relate too well to the local adults. The best solution to this problem is to get involved with children. Service in Vacation Bible Schools or involvement in orphanages often bonds our students immediately to the culture and the people.

Meals in people's homes (even when "sign language" is the only means of communication), serving alongside the local workers, and joint youth-group activities have all provided our team members with a richer appreciation for people who are different—but just as loving and just as committed to Christ as anyone they know.

In our efforts to get to know local people on our trips, team members have:

• participated in African feasts,

• eaten "curried goat" in the home of a Hindustani couple,

• heard the testimonies of people converted from Hinduism, Islam, animism, and alcoholism,

• shared in stories of "God versus the demons,"

• learned that education is not measured by diplomas in some cultures but rather by an ability to speak five or more languages,

• felt what it is to be associated with the "ugly American" stereotype,

• found out that teenagers around the world have some things in common.

Second, love the place where the team serves. One of the errors of some missionaries is that they fail to enjoy the locale into which God has called them to serve. Serving should be motivated by love and obedience, but service does not preclude enjoyment.

When our teams go out, we encourage our hosts to plan at least one fun day to enjoy the people, the culture, and the geography of the land. In Costa Rica, this meant a trip to see the volcano as well as a venture to the Atlantic-side beaches. In Venezuela, it meant a trip to the jaguar "farm" and a morning of shopping in the marketplace.

In many cultures, it has meant bartering for trinkets and souvenirs. In some places, it has led to animal safaris or bird-watching expeditions. Team members have learned to love the land and the people through shared meals, involvement in local parties, and general "relaxed time" with the people.

Expanding students' world views means helping them realize that their home is not the *only* enjoyable or beautiful or friendly spot on earth. God gives us a rich diversity of people, cultures, and nature to learn from and enjoy.

Third, try the language! One of the most evident cultural

distinctives is language. Accents differ from place to place in our own country, and languages vary widely throughout the earth. Yet language is the most basic tool for building relationships, so trying to communicate will help us and our teams express our desire to adapt to another culture.

A greeting in Spanish in Latin America—even when the pronunciation is not too accurate—is usually appreciated. A northerner trying to speak "Southern" is worth a few laughs and communicates the speaker's desire to identify with the local people.

On many of our trips, we try to teach students the basic greetings of the people that we go to serve. In some instances, our hosts have sent us tape recordings of greetings, basic phrases, and simple sentences so that we are ready to communicate a little with at least an approximately accurate accent.

Efforts to communicate are not without potential hazards, however. Sometimes we think we know more French or Spanish (or some other language that we have had training in) than we really do. It's easy to make fools of ourselves by using wrong vocabulary words or mispronunciations. In West Germany, I accidentally introduced my wife as my "Mistress." In Kenya, I picked up a phrase in the local language, *Kikuyu*, and proceeded to walk around saying, "We greet you," even while I was alone. The Kenyans were very gracious, but they did give me a look that said, "Is someone else with you that I cannot see?"

Fourth, go to church. The local expressions of worship, even if they are in another language, are excellent ways to build a cross-cultural appreciation in our teams. By worshiping in another cultural form, students learn that God is exalted in many different ways in many different languages. "*Our* church" does *not* have the only way to worship.

Revelation 7:9 records John's picture of people from every tribe and language and people worshiping God. When we take our teams into situations where another language is spoken, or the people are dressed differently, or the church looks unusual to us, or the songs are written in a local tonal structure, we are getting a "preview of coming attractions," because our cross-cultural worship experience is a foreshadowing of the coming kingdom of Christ.

Cultural Sensitivity

Effective cross-cultural appreciation should not be like going to a museum to observe the "oddities" of other people. We should try to exemplify and teach a healthy respect on our teams that communicates genuine love for the people we visit. (In our training process, we require the memorization of Philippians 2:5-11 because it describes Jesus cultural identification with us.)

Cultural sensitivity should not be assumed; it should be taught. We have observed the following as *basic* to the respect for others we want to convey:

1. *Don't point.* "Gawking" or staring at others, pointing, or loud commentary on some observation is very offensive to our local partners. It reduces their culture to a zoo that we are visiting.

2. *Be careful with English.* In non-English-speaking countries, we have found that far more people understand English than we might realize. As a result, we discourage jokes and editorial comments because they are often understood by the people we are with, and this hurts them and our relationship with them.

3. *Watch facial expressions.* Even if our lips are silent, our wide-eyed looks or frowns or sneers communicate our feelings. Facial expressions communicate disapproval, joy, judgment, and pleasure, and we must be wise in how we use our facial responses.

Staying Healthy

Some readers have already been asking mental questions about health, hygiene, and safety. How can we immerse ourselves in a culture without contracting some parasite or deadly disease? How can we stroll through marketplaces without exposing ourselves to danger?

The questions are very real, and there are no pat answers. There are great risks involved, and we need to decide, before God, what is acceptable and what is not.

One of our summer teams was traveling through Europe during a time when airplane hijackings were on every parent's mind. One parent finally asked me, "Can you guarantee us that their plane will not be hijacked?"

I responded as honestly as I could. "We can never *guarantee* anything like that, but I can tell you that we are in greater statistical danger on the drive to our airport than we are in a European airport. You, as parents, must decide for yourselves what is an acceptable risk."

Parents, team leaders, and students must all balance the realities of risk, adventure, and faith. To help everyone, we publish a brief section on staying healthy in our training manual. (This appears at the end of this chapter.)

Help Students Articulate

Identifying the differences or appreciating other people's cultures is not always easy, especially in a short experience that may last a few days or weeks. To assist in the process, we offer the following sample list of questions that students can ask (or observe) in order to articulate cultural diversity.

1. How do people celebrate holidays? Christmas? Saints' days? Independence Day?

2. Who are the national heroes, both past and present? What made them heroes?

3. What do people enjoy doing with their "free" time?

4. What are their favorite foods? What are the most common foods?

5. Is there a significance to the way people dress?

6. What do the people think about people from the United States?

7. How do the races or ethnic groups within the culture mix? If they do not, is there any obvious reason why?

8. What is the setup of the family structure?

Mark Twain is credited with the observation that "traveling is the enemy of hatred, bigotry, and racism, all foes to real learning." Twain's comments are correct only if the travelers are ready and willing to learn.

Effective expansion of our world views and the world views of our students can result from cross-cultural experiences in serving, but it takes work. The learning will require an appreciation of the cultures of others, a love for people who are different from us, and worship of the God who is Lord over all peoples and cultures.

STAYING HEALTHY
(From our Mission Team training manual)

1. Bring sunscreen, a hat, and keep your shoulders covered when you work. The sun in many of the places we are going is more severe than we are accustomed to. A severe sunburn can incapacitate you for days.

2. In foreign countries, do not go hopping into fresh water without first asking your missionary hosts. In many areas of the world, bodies of fresh

water contain parasites that enter through your skin. These parasites are very difficult to get rid of and could be fatal if unattended.

3. Do not walk around with bare feet. Hookworm (another parasite) enters through bare skin. When digging with your hands, wear gloves, and when walking around, wear shoes, slippers, or flip-flops.

4. Be very cautious about green leafy vegetables. The general rule of thumb is this: if you cannot peel it, boil it; if you cannot boil it, don't eat it! Do not eat any fruit or vegetable raw unless you wash it and then peel it.

5. About water: Some statistics report that 80 percent of diseases in the Third World are transmitted through impure water. Ask your missionary hosts if the water is all right to drink. Remember, if the water is not healthful, you cannot swallow it in the shower, use it to brush your teeth, or have it in your drinks in the form of ice.

6. Expect that you will get diarrhea. Even slight changes in our own country can upset the intestinal tract. To control diarrhea, bring with you Kaopectate, Lomotil, or Parapectolin (the latter two require a prescription).

7. To prevent unnecessary trips to the clinic or hospital while your team is serving, bring Band-aids with you, get an updated tetanus shot *before* you go, and remember any needed allergy medicines.

8. Ask your team leader or hosts about other required shots. Yellow fever, cholera, gamma globulin, and typhoid are the most commonly required. Antimalarial treatment (usually chloroquine) may also be recommended.

9. Be careful with insects and animals. If you swim in salt water, be careful with spiny urchins or stinging jellyfish. On land, tarantulas, blackwidow spiders, scorpions, and "fire ants" are all potential dangers, not to mention snakes. In general, be careful; do not antagonize or attack them. Few are deadly, but many of these creatures can make you very ill. Treat them with respect!

10. While we will encourage adventure, experimentation, and involvement in the culture, we still want to encourage you *not* to take unnecessary risks. You are most valuable to your team if you are healthy.

CHAPTER FIFTEEN
ADVENTURE

Earlier in the book, we discussed the state of young people today with respect to their feelings of being nonparticipants in the adult world. They need to be taught how they can "make a difference," but there is an added problem: many young people are quite passive, not willing to try, and happy to watch others live life for them. There seem to be few adventurers, but many who are willing to watch others experience adventure for them. These students do not seem to want adventure.

The mission-team experience is a crucial environment for helping students break out of their passive mode into active participation in life, and this process begins with the leaders. *Modeling* once again becomes our goal.

Students will break out of passivity into a love for enjoying and experiencing life if they see these qualities exemplified in their leaders. The popular discipleship motto "More things are caught than are taught" summarizes the point. If students do not see our willingness to experience life (rather than sitting back and watching it), they will have no one to emulate.

I have been thrilled to see students gain a more adventuresome view toward life as a result of serving on our teams, but I attribute much of this growth to the "Go for it!" spirit which is communicated to them through the example of their leaders.

One of the greatest tales of adventure occurred in one of our teams to Surinam, South America. Our host, Glen Libby, was very adventuresome himself, so he set a great pace for helping us all enjoy the northern fringes of the Amazon River Valley. After one of our days of work, he invited us to go "cayman" hunting (the South American version of the alligator).

We went out together, armed with his shotgun and several flashlights (to pick up the reflection of caymans' eyes in the swampy areas in which they swam). After several unsuccessful attempts, we finally saw the reflection of a cayman's eye in a huge puddle not far from our car. Glen loaded the gun and blasted away. The cayman went belly-up, and Glen snatched it up.

To our amazement, the cayman was only dazed, not killed. It began thrashing its tail as Glen stuffed it in a burlap bag for the trip back to camp. I was given the privilege of sitting next to the bag— live cayman within.

When we arrived at camp, Glen lined up the cayman to be killed by one blow of his machete. In the spirit of adventure, I volunteered to do it. So, machete in hand, the terrified suburban youth worker from Boston overcame his fears and slaughtered and skinned his first cayman.

The team shared a meal of cayman and rice the following night as the spirit of adventure spread on the team.

The spirit of adventure may be seen by some as being dangerous in a Christian context. Many missionaries will warn against wrong motivation for serving, but I believe that the danger must be accepted in the process of growth. We may have students come on missions service experiences primarily out of the desire for adventure, but we can help them grow in their commitment to serve during the project. (At least they will find out that missionary work does not have to be boring!)

We may also have students who come on a team to serve, but their fears keep them from being effective. Perhaps an implantation of a little spirit of adventure will help these students overcome their fears *so that* they can serve.

What Type of Adventure?

Doubts about whether or not adventure is a good quality can be answered best by defining what type of adventure we are after. Are we trying to encourage a student to be the future "Indiana Jones" of our world or the future "Hudson Taylor"? The type of adventure we encourage is important.

One type of adventure involves *faith*. At the Urbana '87 Conference, Dr. Tony Campolo challenged students with the words of the old "Star Trek" television show: "To boldly go where no man has gone before." Is this the adventure of explorers? Not according to Dr. Campolo. He was encouraging students to venture forth in the adventure of faith, trusting God like the heroes of Hebrews 11.

Missions-team experiences are excellent instructional tools in this adventure of faith because they put students in situations where they *must* trust God. In the safety of their homes, schools, and youth groups, many of our students have never been in a situation where they were forced to trust God.

In the face of personal danger, insurmountable financial needs, and unpredictable foreign surroundings, students on mission teams are removed from the safety zone. For many of them, they are required to put their trust in God to provide for them or deliver them for the very first time in their lives.

One of our teams was in the city of Aachen, West Germany for a day of shopping and relaxation. We split into two groups, and all of the team leaders went with the first group to Belgium for the day. The second group wanted to shop in Aachen so we left them with one mandate: stay together!

In the course of the day, their group got separated. When the group members realized that they had lost each other, they began to panic. Finally, after searching for each other without success, they prayed, each group apart from the other, but both in prayer.

Each group felt strongly that they should return to their hotel and hope to find the other there. When they arrived at the hotel almost simultaneously, they rejoiced! To them, it was the greatest experience of answered prayer of the trip. *God* had kept the other group safe; *God* had brought them back together!

A group from Holden Chapel (Holden, Massachusetts) ventured forth on their first mission team ever. Destination: Appalachia in Tennessee. Little did they know that their greatest experience in the adventure of faith would occur *en route*.

As they traveled, one of the students became very sick—slurred speech, nausea, incomprehensibility. The team members grew more and more fearful, and they prayed!

God directed their travels to a clinic in the mountains, their only medical option at that point. The nurse on duty was friendly to the group; she had studied in Boston at the Joslin Diabetes Clinic. She recognized the symptoms in the student immediately as the adolescent onset of diabetes. The student was treated just before she would have slipped into a diabetic coma and possibly died.

For that Appalachia service team, the miracle of answered prayer established them in an adventure of faith on the first two days of the trip.

Adventures in Obedience

Second, there are *adventures in obedience*. When God instructs us to obey Him, He does not always answer our questions of

"Why?" The adventure of going out to serve in another part of our country or world will include these opportunities to obey, even when there is no apparent explanation.

One of our inner city teams worked in Newark, New Jersey in a very difficult area of that city. The team members were quite irritated by the numerous rules and regulations which were dumped on them after their arrival by the host group. One student commented, "It seems a bit extreme, don't you think?"

The host group offered little explanation to the rules except to assure them that they knew better. One of the rules that students disliked most was, "No women on the porch or outside the home after dusk."

On one hot July night, the women of the team were upstairs in their second-floor apartment, sulking about their captivity. They heard a lot of noise from the bakery on the first floor. It was being robbed by thieves with guns! The students prayed for God's deliverance and never questioned the host group's rules again.

Students also learn the adventure of obedience through their interaction with missionaries. The stories that veteran missionaries can relay can be modern updates of the psalmist's words, "I was young and now I am old, yet I have never seen the righteous forsaken or their children begging bread" (Psalm 37:25).

Adventures in Relationships

Third, missions provide students with *adventures of living together.* Many of our summer mission team participants live very separate lives from each other *until* we go out together in service. In this context, they learn that the greatest adventure of living is sharing life with others.

In many of our most adventuresome experiences, we have had students who were hesitant, scared, or resistant to the experience— whether it was camping in the jungle or eating new foods. They learned, however, that sharing the experience together was what gave them the courage to rise to the occasion.

In a unique way, mission-team adventures create a deeper understanding of the concept of fellowship because students learn that they are dependent on each other and on the Lord.

The great Christian psychologist, Paul Tournier, writes, "Life is an adventure directed by God."[1] Mission-team experiences can help students grow in their views of life and in their understanding of God if the element of adventure is part of the team experience.

In the course of our mission-team experiences, I personally have grown in new ways to trust God in the face of adventure. As a leader, trusting God with the lives of the team members under my care is a constant challenge. As team participants, my wife and I have grown in our faith as we have joined fellow team members in:

• traveling on public transportation in countries where we could not speak one word of the language,

• fishing for piranhas out of dugout canoes on a South American lake,

• camping with our team in the foothills of Mount Kilimanjaro,

• sipping mint tea in the marketplace of Marrakech, Morocco,

• traveling by train across Germany along the beautiful Rhine River,

• standing with a team of 15 overlooking the wonder of Victoria Falls in Zambia/Zimbabwe.

Adventure—it puts us in a place where we *must* trust God.

NOTES
[1]Paul Tournier, *The Adventure of Living* (New York: Harper and Row, 1965), p. 153.

CHAPTER SIXTEEN
MEASURABILITY

In the process of expanding the world views of the students with whom we are working, we want to help them know for sure that they can *make a difference!* In the midst of teamwork, adventure, and all of the other factors of growth, a service experience should also include some aspect of measurability. We want students to see *how* they did make a difference in God's world.

When we send out our young people to serve, we must keep the goal of tangible results in mind. If we conclude a team experience with an encouragement like, "Well, Gang, we were a real blessing to the missionaries," young people may not see this as a visible way that God used their lives. What does it mean to be a *blessing?*

Perhaps it is an expression of our materialistic culture, but the fact remains: *we like to see the results of our labors!* In the past, our teams have been gratified to walk away from fields that they have seeded, buildings that they have painted, log cabins that they have built, and walls that they have repaired.

As leaders, this measurability factor must be handled wisely. On the project, it is wisest to look over the work and to set the goals *after* arriving. For example, if we think that our team can paint one building but not two, then we should set our team goal as "to paint one building completely." If we accomplish this and move on to building number two, our team is an immense success.

If, on the other hand, we arrive and set our goal as "to paint both buildings," and we complete only one-and-a-half buildings, we fall short, and the team feels like a failure.

Goal-Setting

When we are attempting to accomplish as much as possible on our service teams, we keep several key lessons in mind as we set our work targets:

   1. Our young people can often exceed the expectations of our hosts or missionaries. The team to Whitehorse in the Yukon Territories was expected to complete the walls of one log cabin at a church camp. They finished the walls of both log cabins by the fourth day of work. By the end of the two weeks, both cabins were completed with roofing, shingles, and insulation. The camp directors were left only with the installation of the windows in order to complete both cabins.

In general, we have found that our host groups underestimate the potential output of a group of high-energy high schoolers. Thus, we are often able to exceed what they might have expected us to accomplish.

2. *Each project will have its own uncontrollable factors.* This is especially true on international projects where breaking a tool or running out of supplies can slow the work down for days.

High humidity can hinder a painting project. Sickness can incapacitate the workers. Poor supervision may hamper successful completion of the task. These uncontrollable factors should make us cautious as we set our goals.

Our most recent team in Costa Rica was severely hampered in completing its work because their host was quite disorganized. Another team to Mexico was forced to repeat four days of work because its missionary host never warned them about the threat of earthquakes; they had to rewire their concrete forms to be doubly strong. A team to Colombia could not finish its painting because of torrential rains.

3. *Setting the goals should be a team activity.* If the leader dictates the team's goals, the students will not "own" the goals as their own. On the other hand, if the team members cooperatively decide to accomplish a task, the goals will be that much more reachable and satisfying.

One of the South America teams set its sights on completing the painting of a school structure. A few delays because of insufficient supplies plus inclement weather put the team behind its desired pace. Since the team members had decided together to complete the task, they decided together to push for 10–12 hour days until the job was done. The painting was completed, not because the leader was a slave driver, but because the team "owned" the goal and was willing to sacrifice to reach it.

(*Note:* All of this assumes that students come ready to work. If the students come expecting a vacation, they may set their goals very low so as to give themselves more leisure time. The wise leader will have to discern this and respond accordingly.)

Preparing for Measurable Work

This aspect of measurability can be a great aid in confirming to students that God has indeed used their lives. There are some other realities related to defined work which benefit the hosts as well as the team.

First, physical labor projects (which are most easily reduced to measurability) are often the greatest benefit we can offer to our hosts. We do physical labor projects for missionaries who are better equipped for specific ministry. Our team's work frees them to do the ministry that God has called them to. If we can benefit a Bible translator by painting her house, we have assisted in the translation process by letting her do what she is qualified to do.

In addition to this, a physical labor project of short duration (one to two weeks, as has been our church's pattern) is the best way we have found to benefit a cross-cultural ministry without harming the relationships of the missionaries with the local people.

Whenever a team undertakes a project that is more "ministry" oriented (such as evangelistic campaigns, door-to-door visitation, etc.), there is a danger that our cultural unpreparedness and our linguistic limitations will actually harm the missionary's ministry rather than benefit it.

In short, we choose the physical labor option most frequently because (as we say to our missionary hosts), "We do not want to un-do in two weeks the relationships that it has taken you five years to build."

Second, measurability is not limited to physical labor. One of our teams completed a Vacation Bible School with almost twenty missionary children in the Middle East. The number of children, the curriculum covered, and the defined beginning and end of the project task gave them a measurable sense of success.

Another team undertook a Sunday School survey in an effort to assist a struggling rural church. Using informational questionnaires, the team compiled basic information about every home in the community to assist the church in its Sunday School and Vacation Bible School efforts. It was a measurable success.

One of the most successful teams worked one week as builders at a Christian radio station and then another week in leading a Vacation Bible School for Navajo Indian children. The greatest measure of their team effectiveness was the twenty-two Navajo children who responded to Jesus for the first time that week.

Finally, in keeping with our sense of cultural sensitivity, we must realize that some of our desire for measurable success will be much more important to us (and to our Western missionary hosts) than it will be to the local people—especially in a context where relationships with people are far more important than work accomplished.

The team to Luampa Mission in Zambia was our most zealous ever. Our goal was clear: we had to erect over twenty telephone poles and string two lines of cable across a mile-and-a-quarter stretch between the hospital and the Bible school. (The students at the Bible school needed to go to class in the morning, tend their gardens in the afternoon, and study in the evening, but, because there was no electricity at the school, their studies were suffering.)

After two hard weeks of work, the task was nearly accomplished. The poles were up; the wire was almost strung, but we ran into several obstacles. It looked as if our goal—to see the lights come on at the school—would not be completed.

Through some small miracles, the wires were hooked up and at 7:15 P.M., the lights came on for the first time ever. There was a great celebration on the part of our team. We thanked God for the work accomplished and the lights, *but* our Zambian friends thanked God for *us*. We were excited about the lights being on; they were excited because they were happy. On that evening, I saw a clear example of the contrast of a task-oriented culture versus a people-oriented culture.

What if the task is not accomplished? What if sickness or uncontrollable factors are so insurmountable that we cannot complete the job? Is all lost? Will our students turn hostile toward missions?

The goal of measurable results is worthwhile as part of the growing process for every team member, but it is not the hinge on which ultimate success or failure swings.

Measurability is one element that can greatly assist the team in feeling that they have made a difference for God. If it cannot be achieved, however, great growth can still occur. The most important contributors to this growth are the topics of the final two chapters in this section—feedback and affirmation.

CHAPTER SEVENTEEN
FEEDBACK

Cross-cultural experiences will inevitably cause stress, both for students and leaders. In the midst of exhaustion from work, weariness from "learning," and the tensions of living together (often in less-than-perfect accommodations), relationships will suffer strain.

On most short-term service teams, team members may also get overloaded by new experiences. They will enjoy the growth, but the fact that they are getting more than a week's worth of experiences in a week may wear them out.

The strain on relationships and the overload of experiences leads to this essential characteristic of a healthy work team experience: the need for feedback. In short, team members need time together to talk through their experiences, learn from each other, and take care of intrateam relationships (relational housekeeping, as we call it).

In order to encourage maximum personal and group growth on a mission-team experience, we need to provide opportunities for students to talk through what they are experiencing and learning.

Feedback Needed on the Personal Level

John went on a summer team with a group of students who were very different than he. They were experienced as cross-cultural workers; he was on his first trip away from home and out of his own culture. The other students seemed confident and outgoing; John felt intimidated and scared. (He wanted to go home.)

John's growth on the team came through personal feedback. He spent time writing in his journal and talking one-on-one with a team leader. He also made close friends with one of our missionary hosts who took John under his wing, listened to his fears, and identified with him.

On service projects, students should be encouraged to consider the personal implications of all that they are learning about team-work, about new cultures, and about themselves. To do this, they need time each day for personal Bible study and prayer and, if possible, they should be encouraged to try to articulate what they are learning in their journals.

In any cross-cultural experiences, students can rush through their days or weeks without really "processing" the information. Their metabolism, the newness of their surroundings, and the partnership with team members can all keep them from thinking through the experiences they are having. Leaders can counteract this by providing time to think, instructions on how to write down what they are experiencing, and their own personal example of thoughtfulness.

Personal feedback also involves one-on-one relationships. John grew through writing in his journal, but his interaction with the team leader helped him feel accepted in what he was thinking. His relationship with the missionary fostered growth.

One-on-one relational feedback is necessary to communicate at least three essentials for growth.

Growth Essential #1—Affirmation

On one team, the workers were split up on their tasks. One group was doing the "glamorous work" and a smaller group of others were assigned to mundane work. The latter group got discouraged and frustrated, feeling that they were being left out. The remedy? We put two of our best leaders as encouragers in the midst of the mundane assignment to give personal affirmation to those that were working faithfully in obscurity. It did not make the work any easier, but it increased the motivation.

Over the past five years, we have developed a system of affirmation using personal notes. Every member of the team is put on a calendar that assigns one note of encouragement per day. This enables team members to give and receive one note per day. We instruct team members to be observant of each other on the preceding day so that they can write notes of *specific* encouragement (like, "I appreciated how you tackled the digging yesterday, even though your back was sore") rather than generic notes (like, "You're a great guy").

With these notes, the spirit of affirmation spreads, and team members start trying to outdo each other with encouragement. Some students have brought special gifts (like pieces of candy or colorful stickers) to include with their notes. When the notes are exchanged at the daily team meeting, it has the spirit of the exchange of gifts at Christmas.

Growth Essential #2—Confrontation

Growth and confrontation go together. Proverbs tells us that the "wounds of a friend" are "faithful" (27:5-6); they are designed to help us grow.

Feedback sometimes must come in the form of confrontation or rebuke. There will be team members who sin against the team or against God, and not every one will repent immediately. Some must be exhorted to realize their shortcomings and take appropriate action.

On one trip, we were touring through an open market where beggars were commonplace. One blind man cried out to our team with a loud moan. A student on our team who was fond of mimicry repeated the moan to get a few laughs from his teammates. My rebuke was rapid and severe. Every team member knew that he was dramatically out of line.

Most personal confrontations, however, should take place in the one-to-one context. My wife faced this with Karen on another of our teams. This young woman had worked hard to make it onto this team, but her performance on site was dismal—at least at the start of the team.

Karen turned up her nose at the food, worked at the pace of a five-year-old, and complained about everything. The other team members were getting demoralized and upset by Karen's behavior. My wife had to act. She took Karen aside after a team meeting and told her how she was acting. It would have been nice if Karen had immediately repented and said, "I'll try harder." But she didn't!

She grew defensive, lashed out at my wife, and retreated from the conversation with bitter tears. Fortunately for us, we were 10,000 miles from home; if we were not, I think she would have called home and said, "Mom, come get me!"

But Karen eventually listened. Over the course of the trip, her attitude changed. She tried to be more positive, and she worked very hard until the end of the project. A loving rebuke helped her and our entire team.

Growth Essential #3—Care

Each student will respond differently to hardship. Some will get sick and try to work until they drop. Others will have one sniffle and imagine that they have malaria. The best feedback that can be offered on the personal level is love and care for each.

While very few team leaders will be psychologists by trade or training, we will get to see the traits of the home in the students who participate. Some will act with us in ways that reflect their relationships with mothers or fathers. Others will be using the trip to "prove themselves" to skeptical parents. Our job as leaders is to ask, "What is the best personal care that I can offer this student which will encourage his or her growth?"

Feedback Needed on the Team Level

Team meetings are the best avenue we have for finding out how team members are doing. In the service team context, a daily time where the team can gather for discussion, debriefing, and spiritual focus is an invaluable asset for group growth.

Team meetings have assisted us in several ways which have helped us continue the growth process in the team. First, team meetings help us talk with students about what we are all experiencing. Although we are trying to be culturally sensitive, we still will need time to laugh about some of the things that are "weird" to us. Laughing about it together as a team can keep the team from joking in a multicultural context, where they could cause great offense.

Second, the team meeting provides the environment where students can ask questions without fear of speaking out of line. We are always amazed at the perceptivity of high schoolers who, in the context of a team meeting, will ask questions like, "Do Don and Beth have a good marriage? They always seem to be disagreeing and fighting." Or, "Is the way that Brad treats the local people Christian? I heard him call two of the local leaders his 'boys.' Isn't this racist?"

Third, team meetings provide opportunities for explanation of experiences on the team. When the men and women sit on opposite sides during the worship services, or the women are required to wear hats, or the children eat in the other room, our students may not understand without some cultural explanations.

Fourth, team meetings provide the context for group repentance. On one of our teams, we worked with a missionary who was bossy and lazy. By the fourth day of the trip, we were all feeling hostile toward him. At one team meeting, the complaining was increasing until Sally said, "But as I see it, we cannot do anything to change Bill, but we can change our own attitudes." Her words stung us all because they came from a godly perspective. That team meeting concluded with prayers and tears of repentance for our own sins.

Finally, a team meeting rekindles our motivation to serve. The encouragement of prayer together, or notes, or singing can all build us into a unit so that we go out together to tackle the tasks of the day.

Feedback Needed: To and from the Hosts

When we go to serve, we are responsible not only for our own goals but also for the expectations of our hosts. To balance both, we need feedback from them. Our greatest crisis on one team occurred when Dan expected our team to do street ministry, and the team expected to build a children's playground. Feedback was needed to bring the expectations together.

Leaders must also be willing to offer feedback to the hosts. One missionary presumed that our team came with an unlimited amount of cash. In the first weekend of our two-week team, we were taking charter buses around the city, going to museums, and eating at nice restaurants. When he came to me the second day with "the bill— thus far," I knew that feedback was needed. We had been admiring his incredible generosity; he had been spending *our* money.

We paid for the expenses of that first weekend, but then we sat down and went over the budget. Without that feedback, we could have finished the team with hundreds of dollars of debt to that missionary.

Some of the expectations and budgetary aspects of the team can be communicated through preparatory letters, but ongoing communication is needed to make sure that our service teams are being culturally sensitive, getting the correct work done, and striving to fulfill the host's expectations.

Feedback: Use It for Growth

Whoever first coined the phrase "No news is good news," was probably intimating the defensiveness we all feel when criticisms or negative feedback come our way. But feedback is esssential to growth for those on a service-team experience. Without feedback, we will not learn where we can improve, where students need help, and where we can improve relationships with our hosts.

Faithful are the wounds of a friend.

CHAPTER EIGHTEEN
AFFIRMATION

People who come into our youth lounge are always struck by the 20 or more photographs (8" x 10" prints) of the summer mission teams of the past. These pictures always attract the attention of high school students. They read the captions, look for their friends, and discuss upcoming team possibilities. The photos are reminders of teams that have served in the past and advertisements for teams that are coming up.

High school is a time when some of the fondest memories of life will be formed, and one of the functions of an effective youth ministry is to try to help create these memories.

Affirmation of the students who have served on work projects or ministry teams is one of the best ways to enhance the experience and encourage positive memories. Affirmation after their service is one more way that we communicate to students that God has indeed used their lives.

Affirmation Ideas

After the team is back from serving, how can we offer the best possible encouragement to these students? Many have sacrificed time and money (and even health) to join in the service project. How can we communicate that we are proud of them? How can we let them know that God has indeed used their lives?

Affirmation of those that have served can begin as soon as the team returns. A welcoming reception at the church or a greeting party at the airport can provide an incredible boost to weary travelers. As a summer team veteran, I know the wonderful feeling of walking through the exit door of the customs area in Boston's Logan Airport into a crowd of cheering youth group members, church supporters, and friends. It is exhilarating and very uplifting!

Most of our service teams go out in the summer. As soon as they are back, we devote a portion of their Sunday School classes to hearing their firsthand reports. It is our way of telling the students who served that we consider them a priority. It is also a way to let the students who stayed home and prayed know how their prayers were answered.

At other times in the youth group, we include students on panel discussions to talk honestly about their work in missions. In this context, they are able to relate honestly how they felt that God worked in their own lives.

Slide shows at youth activities, paragraphs in the youth newsletter, and testimonies in preparation for next year's teams have also worked as tools for affirming team members. Photographs of the team as well as homemade video reports have all been useful in our efforts to encourage those who have served.

Neither the youth group nor the church will fully understand the intensity of the experience of the team, so it is very important to include postproject time for the team to affirm each other.

On one level, the team can be encouraged by getting team T-shirts which remind them of their team experience. On another level, the team's affirmation must come from spoken words. A note of encouragement and thanks from the team leaders, verbal awards (like the most-improved-worker awards that we have given to some students), and copies of thank-you letters from the hosts can all edify the team.

Photographs in the church lobby, interviews in the worship services, slide shows, reports, and prayers of thanksgiving can all be the church's statement of affirmation to team members.

At Grace Chapel, the fourth Sunday of September is usually reserved for the summer teams report night. There is a slide show that summarizes the work of those who have gone out. The teams stand up front wearing team T-shirts (if their team had them). People are interviewed, and there is applause and appreciation for the work accomplished.

After the service, we retire to fellowship hall to have refreshments and tour through exhibits created by team members. Through the general service and the personal attention at the displays, students are reminded that their church has been fully behind them.

Although it is not always possible, it is ideal if the team can be affirmed by the local community as well as by the church. Community newspapers, local news broadcasts, or local civic groups may be interested in finding out how the teams have worked and affirming them for it.

We did a combined team for several years with the youth group from Twelfth Baptist Church in Boston. The team did a variety of work projects *before* they went, and then they traveled to Haiti. In the overall preparation and return process, the community contacts of the people at Twelfth Baptist led to newspaper stories, radio interviews, and a television spot. The community was excited to send this group out!

To encourage community awareness, we have, at times, issued press releases describing our teams. Other years we have sent black and white photographs of the team to the local papers. Some students have been interviewed in their school papers while other teams have gone to speak at other churches in the area. All of this "outside attention" encourages our students to be those who are active in "making a difference."

In the home, parents are often more willing to give affirmation to their teens than the teens are to receive it. As a result, we encourage students to take it as their ministry to talk through the work-team experience with their parents.

Inviting parents to team summary meetings or encouraging students to go through their journals with their parents can work to let the parents know the specifics of the projects and thus affirm their children more accurately for the work they accomplished.

Affirmation: It's Needed

In a world that often takes people for granted and refuses to say "thank you," the ministry of affirmation is essential. When we make affirmation part of the cross-cultural work experience for students, it is our way to say, "We're proud of you" and "God has used your lives." These are two messages today's young people desperately need to hear.

Section Five

EXPANDING YOUR STUDENTS' WORLD VIEW
Results

The experience of understanding and ministering to young people is full of challenges, pitfalls, rewards, and adventures. In spite of whatever hardships there may be, however, I have found the process of growing with them toward expanded world views to be one of the most fulfilling experiences of my life.

Before discussing the various ways to follow up a young person's interest in missions and experience the life-changing power of expanded world views, consider the following three observations.

First, growth is a long-term process, not a rapid-result affair. Youth leaders who conduct one missions quiz or have one missionary speaker or venture out on one service team and then expect incredible results will be sorely disappointed. The results that we have seen in the lives of students have occurred over the course of *years*, not weeks.

Second, it *is* possible to grow world Christians who are open to missionary service and available to offer their lives as "living sacrifices" (Romans 12:1) to the Lord. Some youth leaders get discouraged because they see students who are uncommitted and double-minded in their spiritual fluctuations. They think that their work is insignificant. Like the students we have been discussing in this book, these youth leaders need to know that *they* can make a difference. All I can say is this: hang in there! The student who drives you crazy today may be driving you to the mission station he works at tomorrow.

Third, young people can be a catalyst to the whole church. As David Howard has said, "When students decide to act, things happen." It may take time, but a missions-minded youth leader can build a missions-minded youth group, and a missions-minded youth group can influence the entire church toward greater vision for the world.

CHAPTER NINETEEN
FOLLOW-UP

The growth in the young people in our group has begun. Through consistent exposure in the church, youth group, or home, their vision for God's world has dramatically increased. Through the positive example of "world Christians" around them, these students are inspired to think about missionary work. The experiences that they have had in missions service have shown them that they can play a part in meeting needs in God's world.

It is very exciting to have a group of young people who are thinking with expanded world views and who are desirous of making a difference in the world. But there is also a problem. For most of these students, full-time missionary or cross-cultural service (or even short-term assignments of one year or more) might be six to ten years into the future. Schooling, marriage, and the repayment of college debts may all play a part in delaying a cross-cultural assignment.

No matter how zealous a student is for missions after a missions conference, service project, or cross-cultural activity, I am always troubled with questions: "Now what will I do with him or her?" "How can I help them to keep thinking with an expanded world view—even in the face of all the delays and obstacles that may lie ahead?"

Whether we are referring to high school students or collegians, the problem that faces youth leaders, the home church, and the missions committee is the same: *What can we do with these students?* Their zeal might be strong now, but how can we encourage them to stay strong? How can we fan the flame of vision that has been ignited?

It should be assumed that the example/exposure/experience ingredients are still useful in the follow-up process, but there is more that we can do. Youth leaders, missions committee members, and other leaders can do their best to affirm, support, counsel, and encourage those who are hearing (or think that they are hearing) God's call to cross-cultural ministry.

Ten Suggested Actions for Leaders[1]

1. Provide individual attention. Make a list of all the students in the church family who have expressed an interest in missionary careers. Take this list to the members of the missions committee so that they can take personal responsibility for one or more students. The individual attention will vary according to time and ability, but the basic commitment should at least include prayer on a regular basis for the student; personal contact (either by phone or letter) on a consistent basis (do not forget birthdays, graduations, and holidays); and personal availability for counsel and encouragement.

As more and more of our students have developed a vision for the world and their part in it, our church's missions committee has responded by the establishment of a special "Missions Follow-up" subcommittee. This committee exists specifically to help encourage individually the students who feel a special sense of call from God.

2. Give special privileges and affirmation. We fan the flame by offering these students as many growth experiences as they can handle, working to give young people special opportunities. Examples include special attention from the pastor, or time alone with missionaries who visit the church. If there are missions experts in the area for a conference or a visit, we try to give these students an opportunity to meet with these people. Our church leaders will get to spend time with missions speakers or nationally known Christian experts, but why not our students? Giving students this same experience will offer them excellent character-forming meetings.

Special privileges should be complemented by special affirmations: a note of encouragement or a special pat on the back for a job well done. This requires some "extra-mile" outreach on the part of the missions committee members, but the personal attention it gives to students will spur them on to further growth.

To offer the individual attention and affirmation, there must be some special training offered to the adults who are involved. Telling a missions committee member to "take a special interest in Johnny" may result in frustration for both parties, especially if the committee member has received no instruction about how to work with teenagers.

3. Institute involvement in the church missions committee. Recruiting students to serve on the church missions committee offers them the opportunity to see missions from a broader perspective.

This helps students to see how missions, missions agencies, and the church all work together. Giving students these experiences and insights will be invaluable to them as they contemplate and pursue their own call. By hearing the call of others to missions (by listening to missionaries on furlough or by interviewing new candidates), students can see the variety of ways that God works. By seeing the administration of missions, they can get an inside look at matters like deputation long before they are required to deal with them.

One word of caution, however: do not do this just as a token gesture. We recruited John onto our committee several years ago, but he lasted only two months. As our only teenage member, he felt uninformed and unwanted on the committee. No one "took him under wing," so he felt useless. No one asked him any questions because the committee members were a little wary of teenagers. He quit, and some of the adult members concluded, "Well, he's just another irresponsible teenager." Their conclusion was wrong because we were the ones who had failed him.

Adults must be willing to listen to the suggestions and criticisms of youth. If their involvement is to be effective, the young person must be a full member of the committee, with equal power and participation.

4. Actively commission. Too often when students return from a missions project or conference, a few missions-oriented folks will say, "Oh my, that's wonderful; we will pray for you." This is often the extent of our follow-up.

Instead, the church must send missions-interested students into ministries where gifts can be discovered, Christian character built, and qualities refined. The church can commission them for certain tasks (within their own church) as a confirmation of their calling.

In practice, this means that the pastor might go to a young person and say: "We are thrilled about your interest in missions, and we want to help your interests develop. As a result, I will be giving you certain assignments in the days ahead to help you to develop a variety of ministry skills. I believe that this will help you to see if God is indeed leading you into His service in missions."

If the pastor is unable to do this, then some other adult leaders should take the lead. We have been fortunate since our youth minister or I have had the time to take such students in to work with us. Some have worked as month-long interns in ministry (where they get some education in the "behind-the-scenes" aspects of ministry). Others have served as summer-long "Missions Interns" where we have designed the program to fit the skills, gifts, and aspirations of the student with the needs of our ministry.

5. *Provide follow-up projects, conferences, or short-term missions.* For the student who is very serious about cross-cultural ministry, we must pursue opportunities to train them in areas that their local church experiences cannot. If we "commission" a student to do a report on the state of missions in China, we are helping to train that student. If we go to a missions-interested young person and say, "We think that you should go to the Urbana Conference, and we will help to pay your way," we are not only helping to affirm the call of God to missions, but we also are showing that we are willing to support them by more than our prayers.

Church leaders may also find it effective to channel students into short-term service opportunities that are longer or more thorough than the church can provide. Organizations like Inter-Christo, SMS Publications, and Inter-Varsity Christian Fellowship (see Resources) are all helpful in this respect.

6. *Guide in reading and research.* Reading and research in missions will help the student to see the hand of God in the history of missions, as well as the trends in missions today. This research might include exposure to missions history and personalities by the reading of biographies and historical accounts.

Students might benefit further by attending special seminars (such as those offered by the Association of Church Missions Committees or the U.S. Center for World Mission) where missions education occurs.

In all of these assigned tasks (under guidelines 4, 5, and 6), the intent is neither to overwhelm students nor to brainwash them. Rather, the intent is to help them to gain a broad view of missions with an emphasis on where they might fit. We need to affirm, encourage, support, and assist in whatever ways we can.

7. *Encourage correspondence with missionaries and mission boards.* With very few exceptions, the average missionary candidate goes into missionary service through some sort of mission board, and he or she works in partnership with other missionaries, at least on a regional level. Therefore, the candidate needs the ability to work with fellow missionaries and with an overseeing mission board. It is wise to get the missions-interested students in correspondence with missionaries and mission boards as soon as possible.

Encourage students to write to several missionaries at a time, so they can get a fuller view. They learn what problems to expect, how to be better prepared, and what the difficulties with people are on the mission field. They will get an idea of what it is like to work under a mission board.

Students can also learn about the administrative side of missions. Information from a variety of boards will give them exposure to different philosophies and ministries. It will help them to understand the requirements and doctrinal stances taken by different boards.

8. *Pray with a worldwide emphasis.* Prayer is the primary way to keep young people in touch with God so that He can direct them regarding missions. Prayer with a worldwide flavor serves as both a spiritual and an educational exercise. It builds their burden for the world, and it teaches them about the world.

Encourage this kind of prayer for at least three reasons. First, it will build into students the habit of intercession. Second, it will give them the opportunity to pray about the world at large; often this will prompt a young person to start to feel a particular burden for one part of the world. Third, this is an excellent way to bring together youth of like mind; this will help them to feel that they are not oddballs.

The mechanics of such prayer may vary according to the circumstances. In some settings, prayer groups meet every morning. Others meet once per month for a solid three-hour prayertime. (A "Concert of Prayer" is becoming more and more popular in many ministries and churches.) At our church, we have sometimes met once a week with these students; in this context, each student was responsible to bring a prayer request for some country of the world. We shared these requests, and then we prayed. The meeting took less than 20 minutes, but it sent each person into the week realizing that God is concerned for the whole world.

One final note about prayer: do not underestimate the *teenagers* who have voiced their interest in world missions. We may think that adolescents are too hyperactive to endure a time of prayer, but this is not true. Encourage and exhort teenagers and people of all ages to join in praying for the world. Since the great need is for laborers, it is mandatory for us to pray to the Lord of the harvest to send them (Matthew 9:37-38).

9. *Train on how to discern God's will and spiritual gifts.* Every person who goes out in cross-cultural ministry must be established in the "basics" of discipleship and the Christian life. Therefore, follow-up for missions-interested students includes training in the spiritual basics. Students will need many hours of personal attention to help them understand how God reveals His will and how to know their spiritual gifts.

We must work with students during these growth years, since adults can be most influential in their lives. Rather than looking to adults for help, students often feel that they must decide God's will in a vacuum, with their thoughts and the Bible as their only resources. The "call" should not come from this type of subjective determination; it should be confirmed by the objective witness of God's people.

Counseling students regarding their spiritual gifts demands that we allow them to experiment with a variety of ministry opportunities at our churches: teaching, or hospitality, or preaching. They must be supervised and evaluated, so they can receive both positive and negative feedback about their gifts.

Training students is a long process. It requires time, energy, and money, but it is well worth it—both for the students who will go cross-culturally in service and for the students who grow into our church leaders. (Some of the best resources in this category are Elizabeth Elliot's *Slow and Certain Light,* J.I. Packer's *Knowing God,* Ray Stedman's *Body Life,* and the books on spiritual gifts by Peter Wagner.)

10. Recruit and send the best. This is the most demanding principle: send the best! Many students over the years will express their desire to serve as missionaries. The test of our commitment to them and to the Great Commission occurs when the superior student, who has so much to offer our own church, expresses his or her desires.

Every organization and every church desires to perpetuate itself. Therefore, when a youth with multiple gifts and excellent abilities expresses interest in missionary service, we may think to ourselves, "But we could really use you *here!*" Pastors and church leaders must set aside their own desires. It may be that God will direct certain students to stay in this country and to work with us. Our job is to make sure that it is God's will and not our own that we seek to do. If we keep all of the best young people in our own congregations, we may deter the work of God in this needy and unreached world.

There are at least three types of students who may express their openness to world missions service. The first is the student who has "thought about nothing else since age three." They are dogmatic about the fact that missionary work is God's will.

The second type is the student who is 50–50; they have never thought about missions, but it seems that gifts, experiences, calling, and desires are all pointing to the mission field. This type of person, however, needs encouragement because there are so many other opportunities.

The third type of youth is interested in missionary service, but feels inadequate, ill-equipped, and hesitant about God's call. Without encouragement, their interest in missions may soon wane or die.

The goal of our follow-up efforts with regard to the first type of student is to offer support and training. The goal with regard to the second and third types of student is to help them to keep thinking and praying about missions. Proper follow-up can help them to see that God can use them and that the church will support them. In that context, we may have the privilege of seeing them grow in their call and commitment to cross-cultural ministry, and ultimately send these young people out to serve.

NOTES
[1]The ideas for this section originally appeared in the article "Following Up Youth's Interest in Missions," *Evangelical Missions Quarterly* (January 1982), pp. 39–44.

CHAPTER TWENTY
RESULTS IN THE LIVES OF STUDENTS

Is it worth it? Is the effort made in youth ministries or church groups to broaden the world views of students justifiable? Why do we spend so much of our youth group time teaching our teenagers about world missions?

Are the efforts made to provide "world Christian" models in the group, home, or church apt to yield results? Why do we sponsor two or three fund-raisers each year for missions projects and ask for substantial aid from our missions committee to send teenagers into cross-cultural service opportunities?

And what about the age-group? Shouldn't our energies be spent on collegians rather than high schoolers?

These and other valid questions have been posed by visitors to our youth ministry, parents, and leaders in our church. I have wrestled with the questions because they address our philosophy of youth ministry and our perspective on young people as participants in the kingdom of Christ.

There are many answers I could offer, but the most significant relates to the changes in the lives of the students. I believe in expanding the world views of young people because it changes their lives, it enhances their Christian growth, and it helps them become the world-aware Christians that our age needs and the Lord commands.

Observable Growth in the Lives of Students¹

It promotes the lordship of Christ. Submitting to Jesus Christ as Lord is the greatest challenge today's teenager faces. Urging our students to consider God's call to missions has helped them realize that following Christ means yielding their priorities to Him. God still uses the singing of traditional missionary hymns and the reading of missionary biographies and histories to stir our high schoolers to intensified devotion.

It instills the Christian "basics." Two-week mission trips have been our most effective tool for training teenagers in the importance of daily time alone with God, the disciplines of walking in the Spirit, and the exercise of loving others. Adult leaders and missionary or national hosts have modeled Christian living and compassion. Their examples are leaving lasting, life-changing impressions on these young men and women.

It solidifies Christian conviction. Many church teenagers live in a relatively secure, "Christianized" world. Through the contrasts of other religions, Sunday School lessons on missions, and cross-cultural service experiences, students see that being a follower of Jesus Christ sets us apart. This contributes to the necessary adolescent phase of making the faith of their parents their own. In the face of different world religions, diverse cultures, and the realities of heaven and hell, students often come to understand what it means to have Jesus as *their own* Saviour.

It teaches students to pray. The "results" orientation of our culture, combined with the pragmatic mind-set of most teens, makes intercession a difficult discipline to teach. By experiencing God's answers to their prayers as they have raised money to feed the poor or spoken through an interpreter in another culture, students are learning to dedicate more energy and time to prayer.

It builds Christian unity. Teamwork in the church is a necessity if the Great Commission is to be fulfilled (John 17:23). If we are serious about expanding our world views, we must understand that it means working together.

Brought together around their common commitment to missions outreach, students who might never associate with each other (even in the youth group) begin to understand the nature of the Body of Christ. Students discover true Christian fellowship through group efforts in fund-raising and in the high-pressured environments of cross-cultural service teams. They bring this understanding back to the church, having grown in their willingness to work together in spite of their differences.

It combats a materialistic outlook. Most North American students are wealthy compared to the rest of the world. Mission trips to Third World countries and educational fund-raisers such as a "Planned Famine"[2] bring this inequity to their attention so that they can begin to make lifestyle choices.

One girl, after seeing a poverty-stricken barrio in Colombia, decided to stop her habit of window-shopping because "it led me to think I needed things that I now know I don't *need* at all." Another began financially supporting a child she met at an orphanage in Costa Rica. Another student who worked hard on a mission team saw how much he could accomplish. On returning home he sold his television set because "I saw how much time I had been wasting in front of the tube."

It creates world awareness. A mission emphasis helps destroy stereotypes and racist attitudes. Students begin to observe the complexities of world economies, and they learn to refute simplistic, bigoted ideas (such as, "People are poor because they won't work hard").

Our goal is to bring students to a level of world awareness that allows them to make decisions about their future in the light of world needs, global opportunities, and their commitment to Christ.

It develops servanthood. Teenagers can be the most self-centered members of society because marketing, the media, and normal adolescent growth phases force them to focus on themselves. Like most youth ministries, we have our share of activities and talks on self-esteem. But we have seen students grow more in two weeks of energy expended on behalf of others than they have in two years of "finding themselves." Many of them have grown in their self-image by giving themselves away in service projects for the sake of others.

It produces cross-cultural servants. As missionaries increasingly work under national leadership, the need for people who understand what it is to serve grows. We emphasize missions with our *teenagers* because we are convinced that preparation for such service must start *before* college or Bible school.

Our goal is for the local church to produce young men and women who are willing to serve cross-culturally. God can then direct many of them to fulfill His plans for our world in this way. Exposure to the worldwide scope of Christianity is causing many to add a uniquely Christian perspective to the career plans they are making.

Why do we spend so much money and work so hard to involve our youth in world missions? Because of the results in their lives. Rather than listening to any more of my observations, however, let the students speak for themselves.

Let the Students Speak

"I wanted to tell you how happy I am that we have some of the greatest experiences—that is, missions trips. This past summer, I went to Trinidad, and I have never grown so much."

Julie, age 16

"Of all of the things that I learned on my trip this summer, the one thing that sticks in my mind is that Satan is alive and well in the world and is doing a fantastic job in deceiving people. [Dan went into a Muslim country in the Middle East.]

"I also learned that if God wants you some where, whether you like it or not, He's gonna get you there. And He's going to provide you with all the tools you'll need to get there. One of those tools for me was the financial aid you so generously gave me.

"Keep it up! Continue to spark young people's interests in missions and in the faith!"

Dan, age 17

"In my time in the inner city, I realized how much I still have to learn about racism, prejudice, and injustice that still exist in our country."[3]

Margie, age 17

"[My cross-cultural exposure] has moved me away from the center of the crowd. I have some perspective now that a lot of my friends do not have. I find myself thinking about the world a lot more. And, I hope, about myself less. As I've thought about my new concern for the people I met thousands of miles from home, I've realized I need to be just as concerned about serving and sharing my faith with my friends here at home."[4]

Jonathan, age 16

"The first way I grew [in our work-team experience] was that I realized the importance of quiet times with God every day. . . . I learned how to put Jesus Christ as number one in my life."

Brad, age 16

"Through this missions effort, I got the feeling that God is leading me toward Christian service."

Dick, age 15

"Nothing feels better than to really work hard for God."

Jared, age 15

"If the Lord calls me to work in the United States, that would be OK, but for now I am assuming that God wants me to be a missionary!"

Kristy, age 14

"If I could become a missionary, I would like to fly planes for missionaries."

Glenn, age 17

"I learned through our missions exposure that it's possible to enjoy life (and God) while serving God as a missionary. (I had a stereotype of a missionary as being a strong Christian serving God in a strange land, always feeling that he's missing out on a happy, enjoyable life.) God wants us to enjoy life and Him regardless of where He puts us."

Tom, age 24 (youth leader)

"I have learned that a missionary's life and work is far different than I had imagined. It's not one or two against a whole group of unbelievers, but a team effort with many strong Christians. A missionary does not just preach Christ's word to natives but can have a variety of jobs. Also, a missionary does not live in abject poverty nor does he not have a sense of humor."

Jeff, age 17

"I learned that the Lord can use anyone and his varied talents in missions."

Becky, age 16

"The basic lesson I learned regarding missions at the last Planned Famine was my responsibility to freely give of my money and time to help those who live in extreme poverty. Because of my involvement in three Planned Famines, it is much harder for me to forget about those who are starving. I thank God for the awareness He has given me of people who have no food or clothing."

David, age 17

"I will continue to pray about missions in Latin America. I wanted to be a doctor and lead a 'good' life here in the U.S., but since I've worked in Colombia, I feel that I'd like to go back and try to help the people down there."

Holly, age 17

"I learned that Christianity is full of startling paradoxes. Before the trip, I was not very excited about going. I wanted to stay home, play basketball, and earn money over the summer. In short, I wanted self-fulfillment. Yet I realized through the service team that, when I sacrificed and tried to serve God and not myself, I found true fulfillment. 'He who loses his life for My sake shall find it' (Matthew 10:39)."

Robbie, age 17

"[As a result of three service-team experiences], I have grown in my concern for people. This personal discovery of my concern for people leads me to believe that the Lord is leading me to serve people through a combination of a medical career and missionary service at some point in my life. I desire to serve the Lord in whatever way that I can."

Jonathan, age 18

"Exposure to missions throughout high school really opened my eyes beyond the small town I live in. It has taught me to stop saying, 'I need,' and say, 'Thanks, Lord, for all You've given me.' "

Bill, age 18

"[In the cross-cultural experience], what I envied most was the people. They didn't have the pressures of materialism or a society surrounding them that tells them only to care about yourself and no one else. . . . They lived each day, praising God for what they had instead of complaining about what they needed. Their Christianity was simple, but deep and sincere. What they had they gave to God."

Holly, age 18

"I learned that the poverty, illness, and suffering in our world *should* affect us deeply. As a Christian, I *should* be uncomfortable with the suffering and the fact that people do not have Christ in their lives. The only remedy—and it's not guaranteed to make you 'feel better' (perhaps more satisfied)—is to do what you can to relieve their suffering. Get yourself to where God wants you to be and *there* you'll find new strength."

Elaina, age 18

Changed Lives—This Is What We Are After!

Our efforts in building the world vision of high school students are not an uninterrupted series of successes. Some of our leaders have been poor examples of missions-mindedness. A number of our exposure efforts have "sunk without a ripple" in the lives of students.

Mission-team experiences have failed.

But through it all, the overwhelming message we have received is this: focusing our students' attention outward has stimulated their Christian growth. Endeavoring to expand the world views of students has resulted in loftier ideas about God, deeper determinations to serve, and more profound understandings of discipleship. These results make all the efforts worth it.

NOTES

[1]These observations are expanded from basic ideas that were contained in my article entitled "How to Shake Up Your Teenagers," *Christianity Today* (September 16, 1983), p. 49.

[2]Planned Famines are coordinated through the ministry of World Vision International, 919 West Huntington Drive, Monrovia, CA 91016.

[3]This quotation from Margie Hanson, a member of our youth ministry, originally appeared in "You're Doing WHAT This Summer?" in *Campus Life* (January 1987), p. 47.

[4]This quotation from Jonathan Green, a member of our youth ministry, also appeared in the *Campus Life* article "You're Doing WHAT This Summer?" (January 1987), p. 48.

CHAPTER TWENTY-ONE
STUDENT IMPACT BEYOND YOUR YOUTH GROUP

After one of our mission teams returned, Susannah filled out her evaluation form and submitted it to me. She wrote a response that I had never received before but which stimulated my thinking. She wrote:

> The trip helped me to get motivated in missions. I hope to go back next year, and *I want my parents to go too!* I think that they would be really blessed if they did.

The feedback from Susannah made me start to understand the impact that missions-oriented students could have in their families, the church at large, and (after they graduate) college Christian fellowships.

If our only focus is to build youth groups with expanded world visions, we are being shortsighted. The energy and enthusiasm of students who are excited about the world of missions can affect many others beyond the youth ministry.

Student Impact for Missions

In our experience, we have seen the world vision of young people carry over into at least four larger spheres of influence: the home, the church, other churches, and the campus.

Dan and Becky traveled on two different cross-cultural service teams one summer. After the trips were over, their parents wrote to our missions committee to tell us of the affect Dan and Becky had on them. The experiences of their children were causing them to think about being "world Christians."

Katie's experience in missions affected her parents as well; they are now thinking about taking early retirement so that they can serve in China in a "tentmaking" capacity. Some parents have been inspired by their teenagers to start building relationships with missionaries through correspondence, while others have followed their teenagers' examples by joining an adult work-team overseas.

Our youth summer team started in 1978 but, by 1981, parents and other adults were approaching the missions committee about the possibilities of adult teams going to serve. In 1981, the first adult team went out. Another one went in 1983, but since then, adult teams have been a regular part of our cross-cultural service team program. The entire church has been affected by the missions-minded example set by the youth ministry.

At this writing, over 150 adults—many of whom have returned to serve as board members, choir members, and Sunday School teachers—have had their own world vision expanded through the preparatory requirements and the experiences of mission teams.

Some of our students and their families have moved away from our church due to schooling, job changes, or family choices. In the case of those who had been "missionized" through the youth group, the vision was carried with them. Students who have left our church to go elsewhere have grown to be missions committee members, missions leaders, and mission team coordinators at other churches. By learning a broader world view with us, they, in turn, have affected others.

I was sharing the concepts of this book at the Urbana '87 conference in a seminar entitled "Involving Youth in World Missions." I had my share of good stories and rewarding results, so I thought the listeners were accepting what I had to say.

After one seminar was over, Michelle, a student who had graduated from our youth group a few years before (after several missions trips and a variety of missions-learning activities) approached me to say hello. I had not seen her in several years; she was in college in Michigan, and her family had moved to Florida.

She gave me a big hug, and we talked about the youth group, missions, her schooling, and more. I did not know that our interchange was being observed by a skeptical seminar participant.

That participant talked with me after Michelle left: "Was *she* part of your youth ministry?"

I responded affirmatively.

"Well, then, *now* I believe you!" she exclaimed.

"What do you mean?" I asked.

She explained: "I listened to your seminar, but I wondered if it could really happen. I thought it was a lot of good theory, but I doubted that it would work. Now that I see that Michelle was part of your church's youth ministry, I believe you. I am in the same

Inter-Varsity chapter as Michelle, and she is the most missions-minded person we have. The vision that she got for missions in your youth ministry is being extended to her college fellowship. Now I believe that young people can get a vision for missions."

Michelle is not the only one affecting her college fellowship in this way. Dozens of others, after graduating from high school, have gone on to become missions coordinators in their campus groups. Their world views were expanded in high school, and they went on to affect many others.

Producing World-Shakers

I once wrote an article on the effect of missions involvement on young people. My bland title was something like "Missions Yields Results." The editors (who are always better at titling) renamed it— *How to Shake up your Teenagers.* Indeed, our goal is to shake up our youth group members into a greater world awareness so that they can shake the world. Let's do it!

RESOURCES

The following resources are useful to the youth leader who desires to make missions awareness and participation a greater part of the youth ministry.

The first list contains books that are useful for ideas or for direct use with young people. The second list contains organizations which are helpful in involving youth in world missions or for providing vision-building resources.

BOOKS YOU CAN USE
Those books which are specifically designed to help understand youth and youth ministry are listed first. This is followed by books that are useful in involving and educating youth in missions.

Regarding Young People in General

Elkind, David. *All Grown Up and No Place to Go*. Reading, Massachusetts: Addison-Wesley, 1981.

Fleishmann, Paul, ed. *Discipling the Young Person*. Arrowhead Springs, California: Here's Life, 1985.

Kotesky, Ronald L. *Understanding Adolescence*. Wheaton, Illinois: Victor Books, 1987.

Olson, Keith. *Why Teenagers Act the Way They Do*. Loveland, Colorado: GROUP, 1987.

Posterski, Don. *Friendship: A Window on Ministry to Youth*. Scarborough, Ontario: Project Teen Canada, 1985.

Rice, Wayne. *Junior High Ministry*. Grand Rapids, Michigan: Zondervan/Youth Specialties, 1987 (revised edition).

Varenhorst, Barbara B. *Real Friends*. San Francisco: Harper and Row, 1983.

Yaconelli, Mike, and Jim Burns. *High School Ministry*. Grand Rapids, Michigan: Zondervan/Youth Specialties, 1987.

Regarding Youth and Missions

Borthwick, Paul. *Any Old Time—Book 5*. Wheaton, Illinois: Scripture Press, 1986.

Borthwick, Paul. *How to Plan, Develop, and Lead a Youth Missionary Team*. Lexington, Massachusetts: Grace Chapel (59 Worthen Road), 1980.

Borthwick, Paul. *A Mind for Missions*. Colorado Springs: NavPress, 1987.

Campolo, Tony. *Ideas for Social Action*. Grand Rapids, Michigan: Zondervan/Youth Specialties, 1983.

Campolo, Tony. *You Can Make a Difference!* Waco, Texas: Word, 1984.

Carnegie Council on Policy Studies in Higher Education. *Giving Youth a Better Chance*. San Francisco: Jossey-Bass, 1979.

Everist, Norma. *Religions of the World*. Dayton, Ohio: Pflaum Press, 1979.

Fullerton, Fred, ed. *Youth Mission Education Leaders Guide*. Kansas City, Missouri: Nazarene Publishing House, 1987.

Great Commission Handbook. Published annually by SMS Publications, 701 Main Street, Evanston, Illinois, 60202.

Howard, David M. *Student Power in World Missions*. Downers Grove, Illinois: InterVarsity Press, 1979.

Mission Trip Planning Pak. Published by the Sunday School Board of the Southern Baptist Convention, 127 Ninth Avenue North, Nashville, Tennessee 37234.

Olson, Bruce. *Bruchko*. Carol Stream, Illinois: Creation House, 1978.

Poyner, Alice. *From the Campus to the World*. Downers Grove, Illinois: InterVarsity Press, 1986.

Richardson, Don. *Lords of the Earth*. Ventura, California: Gospel Light Publications, 1985.

Richardson, Don. *Peace Child*. Ventura, California: Gospel Light Publications, 1974.

Shaw, John C. *The Workcamp Experience: Involving Youth in Outreach to the Needy*. Loveland, Colorado: GROUP Books, 1987.

Stepping Out: A Guide to Short-Term Missions. Monrovia, California: Short-Term Missions Advocates, 1987.

Wallstrom, Timothy C. *The Creation of a Student Movement to Evangelize the World*. Pasadena, California: William Carey Library, 1980.

Ward, Ted. *Games of Other Cultures*. Holt, Michigan: Associates of Urbanas, n.d.

WORLD CHRISTIAN Magazine, P.O. Box 40010, Pasadena, California, 91104.

ORGANIZATIONS WHICH YOU SHOULD KNOW ABOUT
The following groups organize trips, publish missions resources, or offer mission training which may be helpful in building the vision of students.

Association of Church Missions Committees, P.O. Box ACMC, Wheaton, Illinois 60189.

Bread for the World, 207 East 16th Street, New York, New York 10003.

Compassion International, P.O. Box 7000, Colorado Springs, Colorado, 80933.

Food for the Hungry, P.O. Box E, Scottsdale, Arizona 85252.

Inter-Christo, 19303 Fremont Avenue North, Seattle, Washington 98133.

Inter-Varsity Christian Fellowship, Box 7895, Madison, Wisconsin 53707.

Ministries of Penetration, P.O. Box 12629, Salem, Oregon 97309.

Missionary Internship, Box 457, Farmington, Michigan 48024.

Operation Mobilization, P.O. Box 2277, Peachtree City, Georgia 30269.

Short-Term Evangelical Missions, P.O. Box 290066, Minneapolis,

Minnesota 55429.

Student Mission Advance, P.O. Box 712, Station A, Hamilton, Ontario, Canada L8N 3K7.

Teen Missions International, P.O. Box 1056, Merritt Island, Florida 32952-1056.

Teen World Outreach, Elim Fellowship, 7245 College Street, Lima, New York 14485.

World Servants, 160 Harbor Drive, Key Biscayne, Florida 33149.

World Vision, 919 West Huntington Drive, Monrovia, California 91016.

Youth in Mission, 6401 the Paseo, Kansas City, Missouri 64131.

Youth with a Mission, P.O. Box 4600, Tyler, Texas 75712.